COMMUNITY DEVELOPMENT IN ISRAEL AND THE NETHERLANDS

Community Development in Israel and The Netherlands
A COMPARATIVE ANALYSIS

RALPH M. KRAMER

Institute of International Studies
University of California, Berkeley

Standard Book Number 87725-114-2
Library of Congress Card Number 70-632526

ACKNOWLEDGMENTS

My work in Israel would not have been possible without the cooperation and advice of many people, and I want particularly to thank the following who were so generous in giving me the benefit of their assistance: Drs. Joseph Neipris, Shimon Spiro, and Chagit Shlonsky, faculty members of the Paul Baerwald School of Social Work of the Hebrew University of Jerusalem; Miss Regina Boritzer of the Ministry of Social Welfare; Mrs. Yehudith Nordheimer of Amidar; Joseph Katan of the Keren Yoseftal; and Shimon Bergman of Malben. I also want to thank Dr. Israel Katz and the faculty of the Paul Baerwald School of Social Work for their hospitality and many courtesies. I profited greatly from numerous discussions with these colleagues and with various members of the Sociology and Political Science departments of the Hebrew University. I am also grateful for the additional financial support granted by the Keren Yoseftal, which enabled us to interview a larger sample of community workers than would have been otherwise possible, and to Mrs. Shoshana Yovel, who was my research assistant.

In Holland, I was greatly assisted by Drs. E. Lopes-Cardozo and Professor Dr. Sj. Groenman of the State University of Utrecht; Dr. W.A.C. Zwanikken, Drs. J.J.G.M. Vroemen, and Miss Thea Hijna of The Netherlands Institute of Community Development; Dr. G. Hendriks and Drs. K. Laansma of the Ministry of Cultural Affairs, Recreation and Social Welfare; Drs. R.R. Koopmans of the University of Amsterdam; Drs. B. Peper of the Rotterdam School of Economics; Ir. S. Maso, Director, Rotterdam Department of Social and Community Work; Ir. A. De Gier, Director, Department of City Planning, Amsterdam, and Mr. M. Traas, who served as my research assistant.

Finally, I want to acknowledge with thanks the hospitality extended by Drs. P. Roest, Director of the Haagse Sociale Academy, in providing me with an office and numerous courtesies, and the advice of my former colleague, Miss Johanna Renssen, who did much to facilitate my introduction to The Netherlands.

Earlier versions of this manuscript were reviewed by my colleagues at Berkeley and elsewhere, in addition to most of those named above, and constructive suggestions were made by Harry Specht, Leonard Duhl, Herbert Maccoby, Uri Aviram, S.K. Khinduka, David Brokensha, Robert Morris, and Irving Spergel.

ACKNOWLEDGMENTS

While I deeply appreciate the help of all these persons and learned much from them, they are, of course, not responsible for the use I have made of their opinions nor for any of the interpretations given here.

This study was supported by a grant from the Professional Schools Program of the Institute of International Studies, University of California, Berkeley, during 1968-69.

R. M. K.

Berkeley, California
June, 1970

CONTENTS

INTRODUCTION

Among the many types of planned change, perhaps none has
generated as much of a mystique as community development. It is
variously conceived as a process, method, program, movement, philosophy, or profession. Not only does it lack conceptual clarity,
but there have been few systematic studies of character and outcomes.

The extensive and largely hortatory literature concerning
community development abounds in recurring quests for identity,
seeking definitions that distinguish community development from
other forms of deliberative change efforts, together with anec-
dotal accounts of some form of self-help, almost invariably successful. During the last 20 years, community development, with
the support and sanction of the United Nations, has gradually
taken on the character of an international professional ideology
with seemingly universal applications in both rural and urban
settings in more than 60 countries. Notably missing in the professional literature, however, are critical evaluations of some
of its basic assumptions, and constraints derived from cross-
cultural comparisons that might provide a more realistic basis
for the expectations of community development. While there is
some evidence of self-criticism and even disenchantment emerging,
there has been little attention, for example, to the role of the
sociopolitical context and the organizational sponsor in shaping
the distinctive attributes of this form of professionally directed
planned change, as well as in constituting a source of strains and
practice dilemmas. In addition, the relationship between the professionalism of the change agents and the governmental bureaucracies that usually sponsor them has been a neglected area of investigation. These variables are specified in the schema depicted
on page 2, which constitutes the conceptual framework for this
study.

This exploratory study seeks to analyze and compare the
practice of community work in The Netherlands and Israel, and the
key variables shaping its character, role, and influence. In addition to their implications for the possibilities and limitations
of community work in these two countries, the findings may have
some relevance for theories of organization, professionalization,
planned change, and the practice of community development.

The Netherlands and Israel were selected because of their
suitability for such an exploratory study. The two countries are
small, highly urbanized welfare democracies relying on central

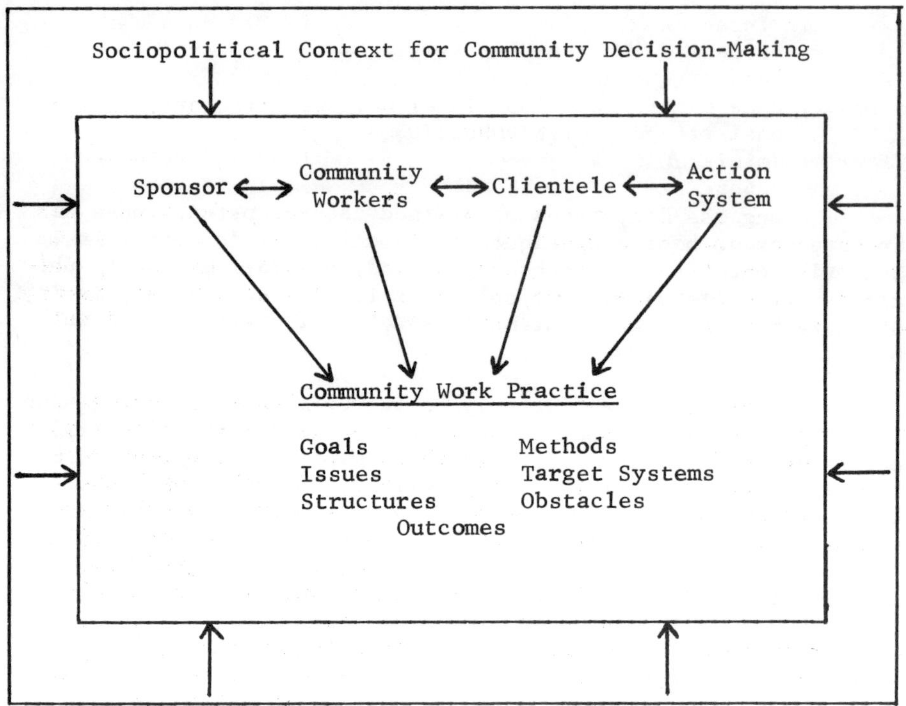

government financing of community and social work, and are characterized by historical, pervasive social cleavages based on
religion, and, in Israel, on cultural grounds as well. The
Netherlands and Israel are probably the only countries in the
world with separate but integrated religious and secular political party systems. In both countries, most of the dominant
structural and cultural features of modernization have emerged
in varying degrees. While The Netherlands is an old, established
state with a predominantly native, homogeneous population and an
advanced industrial economy, Israel is a very new state, comprised
of immigrants from about 80 countries, continuously under attack,
and with a developing economy. Yet the community workers in both
countries espouse the same professional ideology, including a
goal of "democratizing" their societies, and they have all been
influenced by the same American theorists over the last 15 years,
during which community work has been subsidized in both countries. Despite the shared philosophy, goals, and methods, with
their stress on participatory democracy, self-help, local initiative, and community integration, community work in each country,
as will be seen, serves different functions and has a distinctive
character largely reflecting its sociopolitical context and organizational sponsors.

INTRODUCTION

In Israel the primary sources of empirical data were extended interviews during March-May 1968 with 44 community workers, eleven members of the neighborhood staff of the General Federation of Labor, nine mayors, and four local welfare directors. A long schedule consisting primarily of open-ended questions was systematically administered in Hebrew by three trained interviewers under the supervision of Michael Lotan of Sociological Services, Ltd. The responses were then translated into English, independently checked, coded and tabulated on IBM cards, and analyzed. The report which follows draws on the findings of this survey together with the results of my own more informal interviews in English with over 60 key informants throughout Israel, including community and social workers, government officials, and social scientists. Despite various precautions such as pre-testing, reliability checks, and consultation with experts, it was not possible to prevent or eliminate some errors and misunderstandings in the processes of interviewing, translating, and coding. Accordingly, I have generalized from the survey data only when it was evident that the question was understood as originally intended, the replies consistently unambiguous, and the trend or pattern unmistakably clear and distinct. The relatively small number of respondents in each of the two subclassifications, and the exploratory nature of the study, made it inappropriate to subject the data to more detailed statistical analysis, which might have conveyed a spurious refinement. However, since the sample did include 20 of 26 Amidar staff members and 24 of 26 community workers subsidized by the Ministry of Social Welfare, I have not hesitated to refer to "most" of the workers when a particular response was given by at least 60 percent of the sample.

In Holland the primary sources of empirical data were extended interviews with 46 community workers during May-July 1968. (Additional details of the methodology will be found on page 84). A long schedule consisting mainly of open-ended questions was administered by three trained Dutch interviewers under the supervision of Dr. Henrik van den Berg of the Vrije Universiteit of Amsterdam, who also served as a consultant to the study. The protocols were then translated into English, checked by Dr. van den Berg, and analyzed by me.

In the attempt to explain the findings, some of my interpretations may have taken on an evaluative quality, despite my original intention to describe and analyze only. Since this was my first visit to both Israel and Holland, I am keenly aware of my cultural and professional biases and of the limitations of this study stemming from the restrictions of time, language, and access, which militated against a more comprehensive assessment. Obviously, any systematic attempt to evaluate community work must be based on more than staff perceptions, and would require additional and more reliable data based on more extensive observations and interviews with a representative sample of participants, local politicians, officials, and representatives of the various service bureaucracies. Strictly speaking, the conclusions offered here can only be considered hypotheses, tentative and not definitive, and I would welcome their being subjected to further study and testing.

COMMUNITY DEVELOPMENT IN ISRAEL

Chapter I

INTRODUCTION

Israel, like most complex societies, defies classification. Some of the unique qualities of the new Jewish state are rooted in its origins in the millennial history of the Jewish people and, more recently, in the development of political Zionism in the latter part of the nineteenth century. Most social institutions in present-day Israel go back to the Yishuv, the Jewish community in Palestine which emerged under Turkish and, after World War I, British rule. It was during the 1920's that institutions such as the Vaad Leumi, the Jewish Agency, the Histadrut, and the Haganah developed, which provided continuity and a framework for the establishment of an independent state in 1948. (See Glossary of Hebrew Terms.) It should not be forgotten that nationhood was achieved in the aftermath of a holocaust in which over six million Jews perished, and following a war of independence in which six invading Arab armies were successfully repulsed.

The most notable aspects of Israel's first twenty years are the "in-gathering of exiles," the resettlement of almost one million immigrants from 80 countries, and quadrupling the population in the face of the constant threat of annihilation by the surrounding Arab states, manifested in three wars and unceasing terrorist attacks. The unrelenting spectre of Arab violence is a continuing source of anxiety with which everyone must cope, but at the same time it serves as a unifying force in Israeli society, binding the diverse cultural groups together with a profound sense of interdependence and common fate. The military danger is also a tremendous drain on national resources, currently consuming 80 percent of the national budget, requiring a citizen army, and preventing a more rapid development of the economy and the social services.

Despite these persistent strains and periodic disruptions, the state has developed to a remarkable degree. It has a viable economy with an annual growth rate of 12 percent and a stable polity which contrasts with most other new nations. It is paradoxical for Israel as a "developing" state to be regarded simultaneously as a successful case of "modernization." Yet the country's most dominant features resemble those of a modern Western nation, even though there are strong traditionalist sectors and elements existing alongside them. Israel is highly urbanized, with less than 10 percent of its population engaged in agriculture; it has exceedingly high standards of medical care,

literacy, unionization, scientific research, primary school enroll-
ment, and economic and agricultural planning, to cite a few of the
indicators of modernization. At the same time, over a fourth of
its population, both Arab and Jewish, maintain traditional social
patterns oriented toward the past, and orthodox religious ideologies that resist the national commitment to democracy, science,
and technology.

It is within this context of a new state built on succes-
sive waves of mass immigration and facing unprecedented problems
of absorption that urban community work first emerged in the
mid-1950's as one of numerous organized efforts to promote acculturation. Since that time the program has had a modest growth,
and in 1968 involved approximately 50 staff persons working in
35 different localities under the auspices of two government
departments, Social Welfare and Amidar, a national corporation
within the Ministry of Housing.

In order to analyze the character, role, and influence of
urban community work in Israel, we will first sketch the socio-
political and organizational setting within which it functions;
this will be followed by brief descriptions of the staff and their
clientele. The major portion of this case study is devoted to the
factors influencing the <u>practice</u> of urban community work, i.e.,
its goals, issues, methods, obstacles, and outcomes. We begin
with the character of the public decision-making system because
the structure and distribution of power in Israel as in any polity
shapes the boundaries of what is possible.

<u>The Political Context</u>

The outstanding feature of the Israeli power structure is
the scope of concentrated influence in a few highly centralized
bureaucratic and political institutions. Perhaps because present-
day Israel is a very small state, and a consciously created society rather than one with a long history, there is a degree of
authority wielded by the central government which is possibly
unparalleled in any other non-totalitarian state. There is no
aspect of life which is untouched by the state acting either
unilaterally or in partnership with other equally massive, monolithic, bureaucratic, political institutions, such as the Histadrut
or the Jewish Agency.

A review of the first twenty years of public administration in Israel observed:

> The State holds the key to virtually anything that
> an Israeli wants to do. He must have the proper
> papers, the right license, the stamped receipt, the
> official concurrence. No group can exist without

the State's blessing in some form or other--legal
guarantee, tariff protection, subsidy, tax exemption,
leased property, free grants, or public declaration
of support.[1]

Owning more than 90 percent of the land and its resources,
the state is the largest employer of labor, and by means of subsidies and quasi-public partnerships is the dominant influence
in the economic and social life of the country. The major instru-
ments of the state's power are the 20 or more Cabinet ministries
administered through hierarchical structures, with policy decisions made centrally and with very little authority delegated to
local or regional offices. While similar to European ministries
and the federal departments in the U.S., the various Israeli
ministries are distinctive not only because of the unusually
great concentration of centralized power assigned to them, but
also because of the extent to which they are <u>politicized</u>.

It is for this reason that Israel has been called a
<u>Parteienstaat</u>--a state organized on the basis of political par-
ties--and it is perhaps the world's most politicized democracy,
with little distinction between polity and society.[2] Israeli
political parties differ from their counterparts in Western
democracies in the multiplicity and scope of their interests and
resources. As one of the most important subgroupings in Israel,
the more than ten political parties own and publish newspapers in
several languages, operate economic enterprises such as banks,
insurance companies, agricultural settlements, theatres, housing
developments, health and welfare institutions, sports clubs, community centers, and youth groups for party members and their
families. As ideological social movements, they gain adherents
by means of these tangible services and facilities, with the result that members tend to support their parties as voters, clients,

---

[1]Gerald E. Caiden, "Israeli Administration after Twenty Years,"
<u>Public Administration in Israel and Abroad, 1967</u>, 8, Jerusalem,
1968, p. 24. A useful historical and sociological analysis of
Israeli political structure and institutions in English is found
in S.N. Eisenstadt, <u>Israeli Society</u> (New York: Basic Books, Inc.,
1967), pp. 285-367. A more formalized account is Oscar Kraines,
<u>Government and Politics in Israel</u> (Boston: Houghton Mifflin
Company, 1961). An earlier, but more comprehensive and definitive,
work is Marver H. Bernstein, <u>The Politics of Israel: The First
Decade of Statehood</u> (Princeton: Princeton University Press, 1957).

[2]Leonard J. Fein, <u>Politics in Israel</u> (Boston: Little, Brown
and Company, 1967), p. 231. As the most recent and probably the
best book of its kind, this volume is the source of much of the
data in this study.

and fraternal brothers. Between 40-50 percent of the population
are estimated to belong to a political party, and 80 percent of
the citizenry vote in elections which have involved a per capita
campaign expenditure rate higher than that of any other nation
in the world.[3] Although one-fifth of the citizens claim to participate in political activity in between the elections held every
four years, it is widely believed that the political parties have
little interest in and accountability to the voters after the
elections.

The power of the parties is evident in the widespread use
of political criteria in bureaucratic decision-making regarding
the allocation of resources, as well as in the more traditional
area of patronage, which has been refined and routinized. This
systematic principle is known as the "key" whereby many positions
in the government, the Histadrut, and the Jewish Agency are
awarded on the basis of the percentage of votes obtained by the
various parties in the elections. As a result, political parties
not only control their own network of institutions, but those
included in the governing coalition allocate the various ministries among themselves and obtain considerable jurisdiction over
the personnel, policies, and programs of the public bureaucracies.
As described by Caiden:

> The State apparatus is a rich prize for competing polit-
> ical parties to control. The spoils to supporters are
> correspondingly large, whether in the form of contracts,
> jobs, financial backing, or otherwise. Such spoils are
> used to subsidize the party organizations, to provide
> livelihood for partisans, to permit political parties
> and dominant pressure groups to guide governmental
> activities in a way most favorable to themselves. As
> a result, ministries become party strongholds, party
> loyalty is an important qualification for appointment
> or promotion, party backing can outweigh incompetence.[4]

---

[3]_Ibid_., pp. 97-144, and Kraines, p. 62. For some inside views
of recent Israeli politics, see Shlomo Avineri, "The Post-Ben-
Gurion Era," _Midstream_, XI, 3 (September 1965), pp. 16-32, and
Ernest Stock, "Grass-Roots Politics--Israeli Style," _Midstream_,
XII, 6 (June-July 1966), pp. 3-14.

[4]Caiden, pp. 24-25. Also see his forthcoming monograph, _Israel's
Administrative Culture_, to be published by the Institute of
Governmental Studies, University of California, Berkeley. Good
descriptions of the Israeli bureaucracy are also found in Yehezkel
Dror, "Nine Main Characteristics of Governmental Administration
in Israel," _Public Administration in Israel and Abroad, 1964_,
No. 5, Jerusalem, 1965, pp. 6-17, and Benjamin Akzin and Yehezkel

Of great significance in any society, these governmental agencies control the basic necessities of housing, jobs, income, medical care, and education for that portion of the population who are former immigrants and who are exceedingly dependent upon the responsiveness and effectiveness of the social service bureaucracies. The major policy decisions affecting the Ministries of Health, Labor, Social Welfare, Education and Culture, Housing, etc., are usually made in the party central committees and/or the top levels of the various ministries, which are controlled by the political parties. The Kenesset (the national parliament), which is also structured on a proportional basis of party alignments, has a rather limited role as the source of new policy or legislation since it tends to reflect and implement previously determined agreements between the top bureaucrats and their party leadership. This close link between the governmental bureaucracy and the party system has, as will be seen, decisive influence on the role of community work.

Like the government and its bureaucracies, the political party structure is also highly centralized and operates in a way to minimize local community interests. Based on a system of porportional representation with the same lists presented throughout the country, the local and national elections every four years result in the selection of a party slate rather than individual candidates. The consequences are coalition governments, and accountability only to the central committee of the party which originally selected the candidates, rather than to a geographically based constituency. The importance of local politics is also diminished because of the very small size of the country, the dominance of national issues and personalities, and the high degree of economic centralization.[5]

In addition to the government, its bureaucracies, and the political party structure that sustains it, there are two other similar institutions which comprise the other salient elements in the social environment affecting the practice of community work. They consist of the Histadrut, or the General Federation

---

Dror, Israel: High-Pressure Planning (Syracuse: Syracuse University Press, 1966).

[5]Fein, pp. 182-185; Kraines, pp. 217-224. The relative unimportance of local politics and issues is perceptively analyzed in Alex Weingrod, Israel: Group Relations in a New Society (London: Pall Mall Press, 1965), pp. 62-65. A scholarly treatment of this subject is found in Szewach Weiss, "Local Government in Israel: A Study of Its Leadership" (English summary of unpublished Ph.D. dissertation, Department of Political Science, Hebrew University of Jerusalem, December 1968).

of Labor, and the Jewish Agency, which is a functional arm of the
World Zionist Organization. While officially nongovernmental,
these massive organizations, through historical circumstances and
highly complex functional interrelationships, are at least quasi-
governmental. The Histadrut is widely regarded as a second or
even parallel government in Israel, and the Jewish Agency is
itself a formidable private government.

Antedating the state by almost 30 years, the Histadrut
quickly became more than a federation of trade unions, and it
would be difficult to determine whether its economic, political,
social security, or cultural functions are most significant.
For example, it owns or co-owns and operates companies in the
fields of road and building construction, bus transportation,
shipping, water supply, and a broad network of consumer-coopera-
tives, sickness and unemployment funds, hospital and medical care
programs, as well as cultural, educational, and recreational
programs. One of three workers in Israel is employed today in
a Histadrut enterprise, and nearly two-thirds of the entire population are members, which entitles them to the medical and hospital services of the Kupat Holim. This health system includes
more than 1,000 clinics, 16 hospitals, 18 convalescent homes,
and 200 nurseries and maternity homes, with an annual budget
more than double that of the Ministry of Health. The Histadrut
is also a highly centralized and bureaucratic institution, with
enormous resources and vested interests which often conflict with
those of the government or even its own members, particularly
the lower paid unskilled workers who comprise 40 percent of the
membership. The older members of the same political party are
the dominant decision-makers in both the national government and
the Histadrut; thus a relatively small elite exerts great influence over most aspects of Israeli political and economic life.[6]

While the Histadrut belongs in any description of the
Israeli power structure, it has a special place in a study of
urban community work because of its recently stepped-up activity
in certain neighborhoods in which it is viewed by some community
workers as a competing force. Beginning in late 1967, the
Histadrut added almost 50 staff members to the Neighborhood
Division (Mador Hashchunot) of the local Labor Councils in an
effort to strengthen its membership base. Many of the community
workers regarded this strategy as "politically inspired" and

------

[6]Georges Friedmann, The End of the Jewish People? (Garden City:
Doubleday and Company, Anchor Books, 1968), pp. 89-116, 303-304;
Eisenstadt, pp. 38-41, 99-100, 102-106, 186-188. The story of
the Histadrut is a major part of the momumental study of Harry
Viteles, A History of the Cooperative Movement in Israel (London:
Vallentine-Mitchell, 1967).

an unwarranted intervention by the Histadrut to extend its influence into their domain, ostensibly to influence the 1969 elections.

The Jewish Agency, in particular its Absorption Department, which was taken over by the government in 1968, is another major social service bureaucracy with resources needed by many of the recent immigrants who comprise the clientele of the community workers. Funded largely by philanthropic contributions outside Israel, the Jewish Agency organized the immigration and resettlement of almost a million Jews who entered Israel after 1948.[7] Because immigration to Israel has substantially decreased during the last ten years, the importance of the Jewish Agency has declined somewhat, although its "paternalistic attitudes," policies, and practices are often blamed by community workers for the dependency as well as apathy that they encounter among the former immigrants. Like the governmental agencies and the Histadrut, the Jewish Agency is also a highly centralized and politicized bureaucracy, in which jobs are awarded on the basis of the party "key" and with considerable interlocking membership between government officials and the Jewish Agency's staff. In all these institutions the top policy-makers are almost always of European extraction, while the majority of their clientele or members are usually from the Afro-Asian countries.

While the extent of centralization, bureaucratization, and politicization may be quite "functional," community work appears somewhat out of place within this institutional environment. The characteristic values, goals, and methods of community work do not seem to be congruent with the larger power structure within which it functions. For example, arrayed against the highly centralized nature of the government, the political parties, and the Histadrut is the localism of community work, which takes place in the neighborhoods where people live, but not where power is located. The professionalism which the community worker espouses clashes with the widespread use of political criteria in decision-making, and the highly bureaucratized and paternalistic character of the dominant Israeli institutions contrasts with the ideology of community development with its emphasis on self-help and group initiative.

---

[7] Sixteen Years of Immigrant Absorption (The Jewish Agency, Absorption and Information Departments, Jerusalem, 1964); Eisenstadt, Israeli Society, pp. 24-25, 196-200. The best single source on rural resettlement is Joseph Ben-David, ed., Agricultural Planning and Village Community in Israel (Paris: UNESCO, 1964). See also Weingrod, Reluctant Pioneers: Village Development in Israel (Ithaca, N.Y.: Cornell University Press, 1966) and Judith P. Shuval, Immigrants on the Threshold (New York: Atherton Press, 1963).

INTRODUCTION

In contrast to other new or developing countries, where community work is promoted by the central government as part of a national plan for economic development, modernization, or other similar forms of rapid social change, community work in Israel has a more limited set of purposes, shaped to a great extent by the specialized functional interests of the auspices under which it is sanctioned. Because the sponsors have such profound effects on the practice of community work, their organizational character, structure, and function will be described next, to be followed by brief descriptions of the nature of the staff and clientele involved. The goals, issues, and methods of community work as well as its obstacles and outcomes will then be examined, and the various forces influencing them delineated.

The Organizational Character of the Community Work Sponsors

<u>Saad</u>. The Ministry of Social Welfare (Saad), one of eight government departments providing both direct and indirect social services, is primarily responsible for the administration of public assistance, child welfare services such as adoption and institutional care for retarded and delinquent children, and juvenile and adult probation.[8]

Although the government subsidizes over half the costs of public assistance, this program is carried out through 180 local social welfare offices for whom the Ministry provides some administrative and professional supervision for the locally employed staff.

Of the approximately 650,000 families in the country, almost 115,000 (17.7 percent) had some contact with the local welfare bureaus in 1966-67, and over half of them received financial assistance or aid-in-kind.[9] The public assistance system

---

[8] Joseph Neipris, "Social Services in Israel," prepared for the International Conference of Jewish Communal Service, August 19-23, 1967, Jerusalem, Israel, p. 1. See also <u>Social Welfare in Israel</u> (Ministry of Social Welfare, Jerusalem, December 1961); Giora Lotan, "The Social Services of Israel," <u>Public Administration in Israel and Abroad, 1964</u>, 5, Jerusalem, 1965, pp. 48-58; Moshe Smilansky <u>et al</u>., eds., <u>Child and Youth Welfare in Israel</u> (Jerusalem: Henrietta Szold Institute for Child and Youth Welfare, 1960), pp. 202-282; <u>Israel Government Yearbook, 5727</u> (1966/67), Central Office of Information, Prime Minister's Office, March 1968, pp. 236-241, and <u>5728</u> (1967/68), pp. 277-281.

[9] Neipris, p. 2. Somewhat critical evaluations of the Israeli system can be found in Eisenstadt, <u>Israeli Society</u>, pp. 208-211,

13

in Israel, like its counterpart in the U.S., has been criticized for subminimal budgets, cumbersome administration, and inadequate staffing, and it also has a stigma attached to it because of its identification with the "nonproductive" elements in a society in which the official ideology is still a socialist and pioneering one.

The Ministry of Social Welfare has been regarded as among the less desirable Cabinet portfolios, and it has always been awarded to one of the weaker parties in the coalition. During the last ten years, this has been the National Religious Party, a coalition of two parties which has rarely polled more than 10 percent of the vote, even though perhaps 30 to 40 percent of the Israelis regard themselves as religiously observant. While the presence of the National Religious Party in the Cabinet is a necessity because no party has ever been able to poll a majority, it is regarded as weak, retrospective, and identified with a set of traditionalist values opposed to those of the dominant, secularist political groupings.[10]

The relatively low status and power of the Ministry of Social Welfare stemming from its identification with religious orthodoxy affects its policies, practices, interdepartmental communication, and coordination on both the national and the local levels. For example, it is not unusual for decisions on the location of new community centers made by other departments such as Housing or Education and Culture, where the Ministers belong to the same socialist parties, not to be communicated to the Saad when it is felt that some partisan purpose could be served. An interdepartmental committee consisting of the top professional persons in seven of the ministries dealing with social welfare has been in existence for eight years, but its accomplishments are generally regarded as minimal. In Israel, the usual institutional obstacles to inter-organizational coordination are compounded by the added presence of partisan political needs and ideological interests.

---

and Harold Silver, "Developments in Ministry of Social Welfare," Report on Second Year of Consultantship, May 1965 [Mimeograph]. Additional data on social conditions in Israel can be found in the Discussion Papers prepared for the Conference on Human Needs in Israel, June 16-19, 1969, Jerusalem. See particularly the Discussion Paper on Social Welfare.

[10]Neipris, "Some Origins of Social Policy in a New State: The Formation of Policy Concerning Aged Immigrants in Israel, 1948-55" (unpublished Ph.D. dissertation, University of California, School of Social Welfare, 1966), pp. 63-83, 208. On the role of the religious political parties, see Fein, pp. 93-95; Kraines, pp. 77-79; and Eisenstadt, Israeli Society, pp. 291-292.

INTRODUCTION

The Community Work Service, originally established in
1953, is one of five divisions in the Family and Community Service
Department, with the other four divisions devoted to Services for
the Family, the Blind, Rehabilitation, and the Aged. Consisting
of a staff of five--a Director (who is not a member of the National Religious Party), an assistant, and three regional supervisors--
its major function is to set minimum standards for the subsidiza-
tion of community work in 31 municipalities, and to provide
professional supervision for the staff, all but six of whom are
employed by the local welfare department. The professional role
of the department does not extend to the three largest cities--
Jerusalem, Haifa, and Tel Aviv--which have a much more tenuous
relationship to the Ministry. The division has been headed by
social workers since its inception, and in the field proportionately more of the Saad staff have social work training and
experience than those working for Amidar.

Within the Ministry of Social Welfare, however, community
work has not been regarded as a major function or program since
it is but one of many local welfare services which are subsidized
by the national government. Furthermore, there are substantial
differences of opinion within the Ministry regarding the appropriate function of community work, i.e., whether its coordinative,
social planning, or "social broker" aspects should be emphasized.
In general, perhaps because of its relative newness and its ancillary and somewhat ambiguous character in the Ministry of Social
Welfare, community work has a rather low status and priority in
the organizational hierarchy of its sponsor.

Supervision of community work tends to be quite close,
since most of the workers are considered by the supervisors to
be deficient in professional training. Yet the division between
local administration and professional supervision on the national
level is not regarded as a serious source of strain by either the
community workers or their supervisors. While differences do
occur, it is claimed that they are usually negotiated and resolved
without undue difficulties.

The original goals of community work appear to have been
modeled after the presumed success of community development in
other parts of the world. It was recognized that most of the
Afro-Asian immigrants who arrived in the 1950's had little commitment to the Zionist ideology, and it was also believed that
the manner of their resettlement, which was marked by the rapid
imposition of Western cultural standards, encouraged dependency.
Community work was originally conceived as a means of overcoming
dependency, stimulating a sense of belonging, self-help, and
group initiative. A priority was assigned to the 21 development
or new towns to which most of the new immigrants were taken in
the mid-fifties, where community work was to help "make the local
population aware of its own needs and, in doing so, promote the

concepts of citizenship, statehood, and community."[11] A more
recent statement adds three other related purposes and speaks of
"fostering . . . reciprocity among divergent civic groups, . . .
attach[ing] citizens firmly to their dwelling place, and encour-
ag[ing] local leadership."[12]

In striving to achieve these broadly stated goals, it was
never clear whether the staff should start with community interests as they emerge, begin with a survey, offer direct services,
or try to organize a community center. Apart from the lack of
agreement regarding priorities and the ambiguity of these goals,
the development of community work was also slowed by both the
paucity and turnover of qualified personnel. One of the trends
noted was a tendency for the local community worker to take on
the administration of direct service functions after needs were
discovered, particularly in the field of the aged.

Amidar. The bureaucratic structure of Amidar (Israel
National Housing Corporation for Immigrants) is of a different
order than the Saad, although there are many similarities in the
locus, status, power, and function of community work within it.
A joint undertaking since 1950 of the government, which has 75
percent of the capital, and the Jewish Agency, Amidar is one of
a dozen housing and development corporations operating within
the Ministry of Housing since 1962; prior to that it was located
in the Ministry of Labor. Inheriting the assets of most of the
predecessor construction and housing schemes, as well as their
mistakes and problems, Amidar is now primarily responsible for
property management, and is the landlord and concierge for 1.15
million tenants in its 238,000 apartment units.[13]

There is some lack of clarity and agreement among staff
regarding the status and purpose of Amidar. Is it primarily a
nonprofit public corporation, a para-governmental bureaucracy,
or a service organization? Or is it some combination of these?

----

[11]Social Welfare in Israel, 1961, pp. 19-20.

[12]Israel Government Yearbook 5728 (1967/68), p. 278. The
Ministry's conception of community work might be inferred from
the activities singled out for special mention in this issue of
the Yearbook: the development of community centers, tackling
the problems of youth, stimulating neighborhood committees, super-
vising clubs and visting the aged, and hot meals for the bedridden.
The opening statement of this report refers with pride to the
close liaison with various service clubs such as B'nai B'rith,
Rotary, and the Junior Chamber of Commerce.

[13]Ibid., p. 24.

Amidar has three quite specific organizational functions: collecting rents and mortgage payments, selling apartments, and the maintenance and management of buildings, gardens, roads, and sewage systems.

It is in connection with the last function that community work is conceived as a means of educating tenants:

> The government realizes that it is essential to identify
> the civic education of tenants with the national inter-
> est in the maintenance of homes and due care of proper-
> ty . . . . Maintenance is largely a question of the
> proper education of tenants or owner-occupants. To
> promote this education, Amidar employs a staff of com-
> munity workers. . . . It is Amidar--in the main--that
> is the agent of government . . . in setting standards
> of family life and decent society in the reborn common-
> wealth of Israel.[14]

The Community Work Division is not the only agency charged with these maintenance functions on which Amidar spends close to ten million Israeli pounds. The Better Homes Association--Tarbut Hadiur--a joint undertaking of the Ministry of Housing, Amidar, and the Jewish Agency also "seeks ways and means of improving home maintenance" by organizing "Better Homes Associations" and promoting clean-up campaigns. On the status ladder within the Ministry of Housing, Amidar seems to rank rather low, but within Amidar the reputation of the Community Work Division seems to be rising. According to one informant:

> In Amidar they are even beginning to treat our work as
> a show window and to believe that it is important. In
> the beginning the attitude was negative and one of
> mockery, and the big question was "Do we really need
> community work?" Today the problem has been solved,
> and now the question is how to make the work efficient.

---

[14]David Tanne, "Housing in Israel--Planning and Performance," Public Administration in Israel and Abroad, 1964, 5, Jerusalem, 1965, pp. 46-47. Over 100 years ago in another country--England-- a somewhat similar sentiment was expressed: "What appears to be wanted is some sort of bridge by which we may bring them (the poor) over to friendliness, regularity, order, and self-respect, which, as a class, they do not at present seem either to understand or to care for. . . . (Rev. S. Haden Parkes, Window Gardens for the People and Clean and Tidy Rooms: Being an Experiment to Improve the Homes of the London Poor [London: S.W. Partridge, 1863], cited in the Journal of the American Institute of Planners, Vol. 33, No. 3 [May 1967], p. 207).

Community work was initiated in the late 1960's, largely as a response to the rising tension between Amidar and its tenants, growing out of the restiveness of some of the North African immigrants' dissatisfaction with their economic and housing situation, which found violent expression in the Wadi Salib riot in Haifa in 1959.[15] The staff consists of 26 workers deployed in 40 neighborhoods, principally in the development towns. The Director of Community Work is an Amidar career functionary, but the Director of Professional Services and one of the three regional supervisors are social workers. Similar to the Saad, there is the same split between professional and administrative supervision, but in Amidar this intra-organizational strain apparently has more serious consequences. (These will be examined shortly.)

In each of the 18 regional districts of Amidar, a community worker is assigned to the district director, together with a neighborhood superintendent who is responsible for building maintenance and improvement tasks. Authority relationships between the district manager, community worker, and neighborhood superintendent are somewhat ambiguous, and the working patterns vary considerably, depending mainly on their personal relationships. In contrast to the Saad-subsidized community workers, most of whom are employed by the local welfare department, the Amidar community workers are staff members of a division of a government corporation within the purview of a national ministry, and are assigned to neighborhoods by their district directors. Just as most of the Saad community workers constitute an arm of the municipal public assistance system and its service programs, so the Amidar workers are also "functional bureaucrats,"[16] serving as agents of a para-governmental corporation concerned with property management.

Some General Characteristics of the Community Workers

The sample of community workers included a total of 44 persons whose median age was 30, two-thirds of whom had lived in Israel for 18 years or more. All but nine were married and had at least one child; 43 percent (18) of the workers were women.

---

[15] For an account of the Wadi Salib riot and its significance, see Eisenstadt, *Israeli Society*, pp. 308-309.

[16] The concept of "functional bureaucrat" is derived from Leonard Reissman, "A Study of Role Conceptions in Bureaucracy," *Social Forces*, 27, No. 3 (March 1949), pp. 305-310, and refers to bureaucrats who are more oriented to a professional group outside their agency than to the agency itself.

This contrasts with the 11 Histadrut workers, all of whom were older men--seven of them over 40, and four over 50 years of age.

The education of the community workers includes some college for less than half, and college graduation for a third. About one-fourth, mainly Saad staff, had completed some form of education for social work, and approximately 20 percent had some other form of professional education--usually teaching. Apart from some in-service training, only staff members had any professional education for group or community work, since this was unavailable in Israel until 1967.

Eighteen of the 44 community workers were of European origin, with the remainder divided equally between those born in Israel or an Afro-Asian country. The Saad staff tended to be slightly younger than the Amidar staff, with proportionately more women (11 out of 24), Middle Easterners, and native-born Israelis ("Sabras"), while over half of the Amidar staff were of European descent, with a higher proportion of them having some college education. Men outnumbered women on the Amidar staff, two to one.

Community workers born in the Middle East were more likely to be in development towns, while workers born in Europe or Israel were in the cities. Another minority--women--were also more frequently found in the development towns than in the cities.

Despite the general lack of recognition of the professionalism of community work, virtually all of the respondents either perceived themselves as "professionals" or aspired to this status. They justified this designation on the grounds of their previous experience, their knowledge and/or attitudes, although there was no consistent pattern in what was identified as the professional component in their work. Among the "professional characteristics" cited were: an emphasis on process and less on task; the acceptance of all people; the development of citizen participation; and the use of surveys, or public relations. What was consistent, however, was that few respondents perceived their professionalism as problematic or at all in question.

In contrast to these community workers, the Histadrut staff were at pains to distinguish themselves as much more cause-oriented than as professionals. A typical expression of this from a Histadrut neighborhood worker was: "No, I don't see myself as a professional. I see it as a mission. The population does not like to be spoken to in professional terms." Another stated: "No, I don't regard this as something professional but rather as a fulfillment of the mitzvah (meritorious deed) of helping my fellow man."

Most of the Amidar staff had been on the job four years or more, whereas the majority of the Saad workers were in community

work a little over two years. Three out of four of the community
workers did not believe that they had sufficient training for
what they regarded as a permanent career.

Thus the community workers consist of 44 persons, predominantly of European origin, who have lived in Israel for a
generation. Relatively few of them have had professional education, although most have had considerable experience in social
work, teaching, and youth leadership. Most of them have been
employed for an average of less than three years in their current
positions.[17]

The Clientele of Community Work

The distinctive ethnic, religious, ideological, and economic factors affecting the clientele of the community worker are
related to the immense social costs of the in-gathering of exiles
and the uncompleted goals of the absorption of immigrants.
Israel, a very small state based on mass immigration and with a
strong egalitarian socialist character, is at the same time a
highly stratified society in which country of origin and length
of time in the country are among the major determinants of the
life styles and chances of its citizens. Although immigrants
from the Afro-Asian countries comprise approximately 29 percent
of the total population of Israel, over half (55 percent) of
those resettled in Israel since statehood came from "Eastern" or
"Oriental" countries.[18] Because of the profound sociocultural
differences between them and the prevailing European character
of the dominant institutions of Israel, most of the Eastern immigrants were perhaps more disadvantaged than the earlier settlers.
This accounts for the phenomenon described as "the Two Israels,"
widely regarded as the most serious social problem in the country

---

[17]Additional data regarding the community workers and some of
the findings of the survey are in the Hebrew publication Seker
Avodim Kehilatim B'yisrael (Jerusalem: Keren Giora Yoseftal,
May 1969). This monograph also contains the interview schedule
and instructions.

[18]An excellent analysis of the sources and consequences of these
population differences is found in Weingrod, Israel: Group Relations. A more comprehensive social and demographic analysis of
these trends is presented in Judah Matras, Social Change in Israel
(Chicago: Aldine Publishing Co., 1965). The literature on this
subject is extensive; two important earlier works are Eisenstadt,
The Absorption of Immigrants (Glencoe: Free Press, 1955), and
Raphael Patai, Israel Between East and West: A Study in Human Relations (Philadelphia: Jewish Publication Society, 1953).

because of the persistent deficits in income, housing, occupa-
tional skill, status, and education associated with ethnicity.
The immigrant from such a country as Morocco, Tunisia, Algeria,
Iraq, Iran, or Yemen has been described as follows:

> His employment is less regular, he works in less valued
> capacities, his income is lower, and his housing less
> adequate and more crowded. His children attend inferi-
> or schools, are less likely to go to high school, let
> alone the university. His community or neighborhood
> has fewer recreation facilities, or amenities, and he
> is more dependent on the State bureaucracies for as-
> sistance. Finally, he is often regarded as problematic,
> if no longer "primitive," and is the object of conver-
> sion to Israeli values.[19]

While the process of Westernization or "Israelization"
proceeds apace, as manifested, for example, in the reduction of
family size in second generation Eastern families, it does not
seem to have materially increased the rate of social mobility.
The disparity between haves and have-nots reflects persistent and
growing inequalities in education, income, and housing which are
rooted in cultural differences. Individuals do rise and improve
their status over a period of time, but as a group, the Eastern
immigrants are not climbing out of poverty rapidly enough.[20]
Despite the strong commitment of the government to upgrade the
socioeconomic and educational status of the "Second Israel," the
mobility gap is widening between them and those who emigrated
from European countries. While there are, since the Six-Day War,
more favorable reciprocal attitudes between the two types of communities, the Eastern immigrants are still the ones who are

----

[19]Fein, pp. 46 and 136-138, and Shuval, "Emerging Patterns of
Ethnic Strain in Israel," Social Forces, Vol. XL, No. 4 (1962),
pp. 323-330. An extremist view of this problem is found in
Michael Selzer, The Outcasts of Israel: Communal Tensions in the
Jewish State (Jerusalem: The Council of the Sephardi Community,
Jerusalem, 1965) and The Aryanization of the Jewish State (New
York: David White Co., 1967). See the exchange of correspondence
between the author and Shlomo Avineri in Commentary, Vol. 45, No.
4 (April 1968), pp. 16-21.

[20]Weingrod, Israel: Group Relations, pp. 52-56. More recent
data on the social mobility gap was unavailable. While superfi-
cially there may appear to be some similarity between the East-
West differences in Israel and race relations in the United
States, the analogy is misleading. At the very least, there is
a much stronger determination to close the gap on the part of
both the government and the people of Israel.

disproportionately concentrated in the 21 development towns and the deteriorated urban neighborhoods. In the development towns, where much of the community work takes place among the predominantly Eastern immigrants, the unemployment rate is four times the national average, with a high concentration of families receiving public assistance, along with low standards of education, health, and cultural life. Comprising 10 percent of the total population, many of these new towns, located away from the major population centers, are on their way to becoming residual communities, bypassed enclaves of poverty and deprivation somewhat similar to the "trap ghettos" of American cities.[21]

In addition to their relatively lower socioeconomic status, their greater dependency on governmentally provided resources whose bureaucratic character is often bewildering, there still exists among many Eastern immigrants the authority structure of the extended family and clan rule which rejects much of the civic culture of Israel. Surveys have shown that such families prefer strong, one-man leadership to a competitive party system. They are relatively insensitive to civil liberties and express little interest in politics, with 90 percent agreeing that what is needed more than anything else is a strong leader to tell them what to do. While there is other evidence that these people cannot be said to be alienated from the state, at the same time many have really not thought much about the institutions and processes of politics and do not expect much from them. At least one-fourth are functionally illiterate in Hebrew, although 80 percent are literate in some other language.[22]

Most of these characterizations pertain mainly to the immigrant generation itself, and much less so to their offspring, who have been exposed to some schooling and particularly the army, which is one of the major socializing institutions in Israel. The effects of the school system, unfortunately, are lessened because of the much smaller proportion of children from Eastern families who attend high school and the universities,

---

[21]"Manpower in Development Towns" (State of Israel, Ministry of Labor, Manpower Planning Authority, December 1964); "Internal Migration," Part 1 (Central Bureau of Statistics, Jerusalem, 1965; Population and Housing Census Publication No. 19). The most detailed account in English and German is Erika Spiegel, New Towns in Israel: Urban and Regional Planning and Development (Stuttgart/Bern: Karl Kramer Verlag, 1966). Erik Cohen has made numerous sociological studies of development towns. See his "Social Images in an Israeli Development Town," Human Relations, Vol. 21, No. 2 (May 1968), pp. 163-176.

[22]Fein, pp. 41, 139-143.

despite educational policies, priorities, and subsidies to rectify this situation.

In addition to these cultural factors, Israelis are further divided along religious lines. For a variety of historical and political reasons, orthodoxy is the only officially recognized form of the Jewish religion. While perhaps less than one-fourth of the population may be observant and less than 12 percent of the electorate vote for the National Religious Party, the rabbinical courts have sole jurisdiction over civil laws pertaining to the personal status of all Israeli Jews (marriage, divorce, adoption, guardianship, etc.). In addition, the orthodox groups have been able to impose their norms regarding dietary laws and observance of the Sabbath and other religious holidays on the whole population with the sanction of the government, which is understandably anxious to avoid a _Kulturkampf_. Periodically, the powers of the orthodox religious elements in the Ministries of Religious Affairs or the Interior, which they control, are challenged, but with little effect.[23]

Proportionally more of the Afro-Asian than European immigrants are orthodox. Both share a zealous commitment to strict observance of the Law and a reluctance to associate with the nonreligious elements of the population. The orthodox tradition thus tends to be quite rigid, autocratic, and a major force polarizing Israelis.

It is, however, not only the absence of a democratic tradition among much of its clientele that limits the citizen-participation goals of community work. Community work is practiced in a setting marked by the relative absence of pressure and interest groups outside the regular political structure. These are part of the highly centralized character of Israeli life and the pervasive influence of government which heighten feelings of dependence and impotence in influencing the established institutions, and constitute formidable obstacles to the community worker in his attempts to transform his clientele into a constituency.

---

[23]Eisenstadt, _Israeli Society_, pp. 220-221, 309-320, 379-380; Fein, pp. 48-52; G. Friedmann, pp. 178-221.

Chapter II

ANALYSIS OF COMMUNITY WORK PRACTICE

<u>Goals</u>

Community work practice, the dependent variable in this
study, will be examined in terms of five interrelated dimensions
which can be analytically distinguished as goals, issues, methods,
obstacles, and outcomes. After describing these aspects of practice, the effects of each of the four independent variables--
sponsor, staff, clientele, and the political system--will be
sketched.

To speak of the goals of urban community work is to specify the explicit and implicit changes in attitudes, behavior,
relationships, conditions, policies, and/or practices which are
sought. Modifications in any one or more of these objectives
comprise the purpose and function of community work conceived as
a process or method of planned change.

Four community work goals were identified in the course
of this study, two of which were directed at the clientele and
two at bureaucratic organizations which serve them:

(1) To educate former immigrants to modify socially unde-
    sirable living habits and to accept such values as
    cleanliness, respect for and maintenance of property,
    and volunteer participation.[1]

(2) To bring different ethnic and religious groups together
    to improve their social relationships and to develop
    citizen participation.

(3) To stimulate more effective service delivery and the
    development of needed social service programs by
    prodding the bureaucracies on behalf of neglected
    groups such as the aged, children, and youth.

---

[1] As one community worker put it: "To try to educate them to
understand the need for organization in order to change the looks
of the <u>shikun</u> . . . to teach them that you can't receive without
paying, and to explain how one must behave."

24

    (4) To convene local agencies to encourage better communication and coordination.

In addition, there was a fifth goal found only in Jerusalem in which community work sought to become more of a nonpartisan political force in the community through various forms of social action.

Both the first and second goals are essentially concerned with acculturation, involving processes of adult socialization over which community work has no monopoly. As educational objectives, they are part of the national goals of integrating and absorbing immigrants and "making Israelis out of them." The third and fourth goals express forms of social brokerage and social planning, respectively. In actual practice, the first goal is stressed somewhat more by Amidar and the third by the Saad community workers, with the second and fourth being secondary goals for both organizations. Furthermore, the respective short-run tangible goals for each sponsor prevail over the usual concern with a long-range process of community development, which might increase the collaborative capacity of the client system.

The sponsors of community work as part of the governmental apparatus are concerned with the Israelization of the immigrant, not only as an intrinsic value, but also as a means of facilitating the accomplishment of their specialized program or functional interests. The mandate of community work can therefore be conceived as including the development of <u>better citizens, clients, or tenants,</u> and <u>improved social services.</u> It involves getting the other bureaucracies to function more efficiently and effectively, i.e., to get them to do what they are supposed to do, not something different. As expressed by one community worker: "Because I represent an agency I can't oppose another agency. The political structure in Israel does not allow the community worker to be aggressive toward agencies."

Reinforced by the diverse cultural backgrounds and relatively disadvantaged conditions of its clientele, the characteristic goals and style of community work thus tend to be much more in the direction of social control and system maintenance than social change. Another way of describing the goals of community work is that they are concerned with individual rather than group mobility, i.e., with altering the behavior of persons in the client system more than the bureaucratic systems that impinge upon them.[2] Some evidence for this focus on changing people

____

[2] On the distinction between individual and group mobility goals, see Arthur Blum, Magdalena Miranda, and Maurice Meyer, "Goals and Means for Social Change" in John B. Turner, ed., <u>Neighborhood Organization for Community Action</u> (New York: National Association of Social Workers, 1968), pp. 107-108.

rather than policies or systems is found in the belief of many
community workers that one of the underlying purposes of their
work is to "cool off" possibly troublesome population groups,
discouraging protests by blunting the edges of controversy and
minimizing the possibility of conflict.[3] Some support for this
point of view can be found in the early history of community
work, in which priority was given to the development towns by
the Ministry of Social Welfare in its concern to help the immigrants who had been resettled there to express themselves in
more "constructive" ways than in the increasingly disruptive
forms of protest which occurred toward the end of the 1950's.
This was similar to the decision of Amidar to inaugurate community work following a growing deterioration in tenant relations
at about the same time.

While the goals of community work are compatible with the
ideology of community development as professed by most of the
staff, with its emphasis on the process of participation, there
is, however, a strain between the priority of task and process,
organizational and professional goals, which is much more noticeable for Amidar than for Saad workers. The community work staff
in Amidar believe that they have been quite successful in getting
formal acceptance of goals which are broader than the narrow
focus on the problems of <u>shikun</u> (housing) maintenance which are
usually of primary importance to the district managers. Indeed,
some of the staff describe their purpose as "protecting the
tenant from Amidar." They place a lower priority than the administration on the objectives of better maintenance, low repair
budgets, and high rates of flat purchases, and regard the client
more as a citizen and less as a tenant. The staff's goals are
both more ambiguous and open, with greater emphasis on initiating
a process of involvement, taking one's cue from client-expressed
needs, and "working with people where they are." Somewhat opposed
to this point of view are officials of the Ministry of Social
Welfare and the Histadrut, as well as a few Amidar staff members
who believe that the community workers should restrict themselves
solely to issues directly related to housing, on the grounds
that they have no sanction for any other type of intervention,
and that unless this were stipulated, there would be no boundaries
to their activities. However, most of the Amidar community
workers do not want to function merely as agents of the landlord,

---

[3]This use of community organization by bureaucracies as a means
of exerting control over their clientele and producing "political
desocialization" is perceptively analyzed by Richard A. Cloward
and Frances Pivan, "The Professional Bureaucracies: Benefit
Systems as Influence Systems" in Ralph M. Kramer and Harry Specht,
eds., <u>Readings in Community Organization Practice</u> (Englewood
Cliffs: Prentice-Hall, Inc., 1969), pp. 359-371.

and so they operate with a much broader conception of their goals, explaining that even with housing as a focus, no phase of the life of their clientele is excluded. As one of them puts it: "I don't think people understand the complete meaning of community work when they try to narrow it down to the problems of Amidar alone." A similar point of view is expressed by another worker:

> I wanted to see immediate results in my work concerning the housing situation. I worked for a year and realized that it was impossible to be concerned just with housing, because it included many problems. I finally achieved success in establishing some youth clubs.

Although almost half of the Amidar workers acknowledged differences between their conception of community work goals and those of the district manager, most did not regard it as a serious constraint and thought they were able to cope with it effectively.

> Several of the community workers expressed their relationship to the district manager in these terms:

> He accepts blindly all that is done, mostly because of our common background and the help I gave him in his adjustment to the work.

> He has no idea of what we have to do. More specifically, he accepts what we are doing and doesn't try to interfere.

At the same time there is evidence that about half of the district managers are either fearful of or not supportive of community work and its more people-centered aims, in contrast to their building-centered goals.[4]

> Some differences in goals between the community workers and their sponsor, which are much more marked among Amidar than Saad staff, are illustrated by the strains surrounding the implementation of policies pertaining to (a) the promotion of the sale of flats, (b) the encouragement of tenants to remain in development towns, and (c) the "Westernization" of immigrants. In each of these three areas of conflict, a question of dual loyalty arises for the community worker: to whom does he have the primary responsibility—to Amidar or to the individual family,

---

[4]One source of conflict may be the fact that there is a very small salary differential between the district managers and the Amidar community workers, even though the former have a substantial degree of administrative responsibility, while the latter often appear to "just go around talking to people."

which is often his client-system (rather than a community, an organization, or a group).

As previously noted, Amidar is anxious to sell rather than rent flats for two reasons: (1) sales relieve it of the landlord's responsibility for maintenance and repair, and put it in a better budgetary position within the Ministry of Housing; (2) home ownership has public relations value as evidence of a stake in the community. Many of the community workers, however, are not sympathetic to the "hard-sell" on what appear to be easy credit terms. They are aware of the hardships endured by families who were pressured into assuming obligations which they really could not afford, with their monthly payments almost doubling when they gave up their heavily subsidized rents in order to get a slightly better apartment.[5] Despite this, the Amidar community workers cannot openly oppose the national policy of promoting home ownership.

A second conflict emerges around the prevention of geographic mobility, particularly in the development towns, and is related to the way in which housing has been used as an instrument of a population dispersal policy. The government and the Jewish Agency have tried to provide inducements for immigrants to remain in the development towns to which they were brought, usually directly from ships after arriving in Israel. Financial or housing assistance is rarely given to families if they decide to relocate. Despite these sanctions, tens of thousands of persons have left the towns, mainly for economic reasons, preferring to take their chances and settle in one of the larger towns or cities. Community workers are expected to help implement this policy of discouraging mobility, and they often rationalize their endeavors by stating that they are helping to improve the character of the environment and give the residents more of an incentive to remain in the community.

There are numerous instances of conflict between the defense and economic interests of the state in population dispersal, and the interests of a family in leaving a development town, with community workers in the middle, torn between the two. Some say that the community workers are like all other Israeli bureaucrats: they identify with their organizational sponsor, and defend their clients' interests only if the latter do not conflict with those of the larger society whose goals are their

---

[5]The proportion of monthly income needed for the costs of housing can increase from 7-12 percent to 30 percent when a wage-earning family moves from a minimum level apartment (48-64 square meters) to a larger unit (65-90 square meters). See Tanne, pp. 42-43.

professional mandate. While both Saad and Amidar workers are expected to discourage mobility, conflict occurs more often among the latter, where the community workers may be held more directly responsible for controlling turnover in the <u>shikun</u> (housing project).

A third goal conflict between organization and professional values for community workers pertains to the attempts to make Israelis out of the immigrants, who have come from 80 different countries. The community worker in this situation is again in the middle. He is sensitive to the culture of the Afro-Asian immigrants and is keenly aware of their difficulties in adjusting to the twin crises of resettlement and modernization. Some of the workers interviewed complained that Amidar wants to "Western-ize" the former inhabitants of the <u>mellahs</u> of Casablanca and Marrakesh, and "make nice, middle-class Europeans out of them." Although most of the Amidar workers are of European descent them-selves, some view their organization's goals as a form of "cul-tural colonialism" and chafe at their responsibility to bring these "primitives" into the twentieth century.

While a few community workers may be uncomfortable in this socialization role, most of the others who have a stronger commitment to the traditional Zionist ideology are much less troubled, and believe that there is no incompatibility between their professional commitment to self-determination and the goals of Israelization. In Israel it is expected that all professionals, including teachers, social workers, and nurses, as well as polit-ical functionaries, will perform a socializing function, teaching desired values and appropriate behavior. While questions have been raised regarding the rate of change expected and the lack of respect for some of the "Oriental" traditions brought to Israel, the matter seems quite settled, even though there are still many social costs to be reckoned. Actually, the decision that Israel would become a modern welfare democracy, oriented toward the West and its technology, was made long ago. There is considerable evidence that once the opportunity is presented to new immigrants, most of them, particularly the young, will opt for this new way of life.[6] It is also true that there is really not much of an alternative, since the dominant institutions of the society and polity are so thoroughly Western in character, even though Israel is a highly stratified society with many ethnic and religious enclaves.

In sharp contrast to the existence of some strain between their sponsor's mandate and some of the community workers'

---

[6]Weingrod, <u>Reluctant Pioneers</u>, pp. 167-204, and <u>Israel: Group Relations</u>, pp. 74-80.

professional values concerning property ownership, geographical
mobility, and Israelization, there are no conflicts at all among
the Histadrut workers. They express an unequivocal identification
with and strong commitment to the goals of their organization,
and see themselves helping build an Israeli society in conformance
with the socialist ideology of their sponsor: "The goal of the
Histadrut is to build a different, a just society." Accordingly,
they try to "guide and educate" members according to the direc-
tives given them by the Histadrut leadership, and they are
evaluated on the degree to which they have strengthened the
organization.

In summary, the broad, long-range goals of community
work are rooted in the social requirements for acculturation, and
are oriented more toward changing individuals than organizations.
There is some conflict between professional and bureaucratic
goals, but this is problematic for only about half of the workers,
mainly those in Amidar.[7]

Issues

The goals of community work generate the issues around
which people are organized. An analysis of the "recent characteristic projects" described by the community workers reveals a
wide range of projects, with considerable differences between
those sponsored by the Ministry of Social Welfare and Amidar.
Substantively, the most frequently reported project of the Amidar
staff was the organization of a House Committee with primary concern for certain maintenance problems in the shikun such as
cleanliness, garbage collection, payment of utilities, etc. An
example of this is the following:

> There was this problem of cleanliness of the courtyards
> and entrances. Those who were supposed to take care
> of the courtyards tried to explain to the people, but
> to no avail. We chose one to be responsible for each
> entrance, and now we are trying to broaden their
> responsibility. Through this committee we are trying
> to create contact between the people and the agencies.
> There is a monthly meeting with me, the head of the

---

[7]A somewhat similar strain between organizational and staff
goals is found in urban renewal, where the authorities tend to
stress quick results while community workers aim at long-term
educational goals (Report on Urban Development--Implications for
Social Welfare, submitted by the Israel National Committee for
Social Service in cooperation with the Ministry of Social Welfare
to the Thirteenth International Conference of Social Work,
Washington, 1966 [Jerusalem, July 1966], pp. 53-54).

committee, and those who are responsible for the
cleaning.

These committees, whether organized on a block or neighborhood
basis, are regarded by the staff as a potential organizational
structure to seek other benefits such as centers, playgrounds,
language classes, and as a means of dealing with the special
problems of children and youth.

Whereas the Amidar community workers were typically involved with the creation of a new neighborhood-based tenant association, i.e., an organizational _structure_, the most frequently
reported activities of the Saad staff were the establishment of
new _facilities_, such as a community center or a new social service
program such as meals-on-wheels for the elderly. As described by
two different workers:

> I helped eetablish a _moadon_ [center] for the elderly.
> The project was comparatively easy and I could suc-
> ceed. This was important, for I had just arrived,
> and it would be a good way to create a relationship
> with the people. There was a survey and we found
> out who wanted to participate. Furniture and money
> were obtained and it worked.

> Several organizations had to cooperate in order to
> get a _moadon_ for the elderly. I got the place, and
> Amidar and Saad participated with furniture and a
> budget. We conducted a survey of the elderly, with
> the help of volunteers and also a nearby teachers'
> seminary. One class adopted the center.

Other typical projects carried out usually by ad hoc
groups were concerned with the prevention of school dropouts,
delinquency, or the establishment of a recreation or cultural
program. Almost all the projects mentioned were relatively
small-scale improvements within a circumscribed geographic area
and involved tangible amenities and housekeeping matters which
were not particularly controversial.

Where did these projects come from? How did the issues
arise? Who defined them as the problem-to-be-worked-on, the con-
dition-to-be-changed? Most likely these issues were based on
needs defined by the Saad or Amidar, who have special interests
in property management and social service program development respectively. At the very least, it is not coincidental that the
community "needs" discovered and issues selected by the community
workers are congruent with their sponsor's definition of need.[8]

––––––––––––––

[8]Community work goals can be conceptualized as the product of
an interaction between the interests of the organization, the

This does not mean that these needs were not "felt" by some of
the residents, or that these issues were "imposed" by external
agents. Because the range of "felt needs" is very great in this
relatively deprived population which lacks many amenities, practically any tangible improvement in its living conditions can be
regarded as meeting a need.[9] One could safely say, however, that
the needs identified by the community workers may not have been
clearly expressed or, more certainly, not given the same priority
by the clientele. The difference in priorities is suggested by
the frequency of the community worker's complaints about the
difficulties in sustaining participation after the House Committee
has been elected or the community center is established. It is
possible that if these projects were more firmly rooted in the
wishes of the residents there would be stronger incentives to
participate. Some evidence that it may be fortuitous if the
priorities of sponsor and clientele coincide can be gleaned from
public opinion data derived from an international comparative
survey conducted by Hadley Cantril in the early 1960's. Heading
the list of types of personal aspirations in Israel were economic
goals, expressed by 80 percent of a representative sample of the
population. This was followed by family (76 percent), health
(47 percent), job or work situation (35 percent). In expressing
their personal worries and fears, Israelis most often mentioned
health and economic matters (58 and 55 percent respectively),

---

worker, and the clientele. What is being asserted here is that
the goals and needs of the sponsoring organization and the community worker seem to be more determining than those of the
clientele. This finding contrasts with the usual neglect of
the role of the sponsor in most of the literature on community
development. For example, the sponsor's role as it may affect
the personal image of the community development agent is regarded as "least significant" in Arthur H. Niehoff, ed., A Case
Book of Social Change (Chicago: Aldine Publishing Co., 1966),
p. 15. A more realistic evaluation is that of Lloyd Ohlin:
"In organizing the unorganized, the interests of the sponsoring
organization determine selection of participants, form of organization, specification of objectives and control of activities. . . ." ("Urban Community Development" in Kramer and
Specht, p. 246).

[9]A typical survey of needs and proposed projects for a develop-
ment town is contained in Joseph Hodara, "Patterns of Action for
a Demonstration Program in Beit Shemesh and Netivot" (Henrietta
Szold Institute, National Institute for Research and Behavioral
Sciences, Jerusalem, September 1967). The results of two years'
work are summarized in Dov Ancona, "The Beth Shemesh and Netivot
Demonstration Project as a Local Enterprise and as a Pilot
Project" (Jerusalem, August 1969).

followed by family matters (44 percent).[10] It is noteworthy
that few of these concerns are reflected in the projects promoted
by the community workers.

Further evidence of the important role of the sponsor in
affecting the perception of needs and priorities is suggested by
the characteristic propensity of the staff members to define as
"community problems" those with which they are working. Economic
problems, which are generally recognized as perhaps the most
serious ones in the communities in which they are working, were
the second most frequently mentioned by the staff, and were rarely
cited as the first problem. Economic problems were cited by only
seven of 20 Amidar workers, who mentioned the maintenance problems
of the shikun most often as a "major community problem." Saad
workers most often cited various facility lacks as the chief community problem--e.g., transportation, schools, day-care centers,
playgrounds, sports fields, community centers, lighting, phones,
movies, coffee houses--as well as a lack of physicians. Mentioned
second was the inability of immigrants to work together, and in
third place, their lack of opportunity to earn sufficient income.

The following are some typical responses in which major
community problems are identified:

> Problems with youth and elderly people. The youth have
> no playgrounds and centers, and the elderly lack social
> life. There are problems in the high school. It has
> existed for eight years and has not graduated even one
> class because the parents want to get their children
> out of this community.

> An out-of-the-way settlement which was never really
> organized or planned. There are not enough sources
> of income, insufficient professional manpower. The
> population is too homogeneous. It has a low cultural
> level and almost half has never finished elementary
> school.

> No communication between the old and new immigrants.
> Children come to school with different levels and
> cultural backgrounds.

---

[10]Hadley Cantril, The Pattern of Human Concerns (New Brunswick,
N.J.: Rutgers University Press, 1965), pp. 99-103. Note that
Cantril's sample is not necessarily congruent with that of the
clientele of the community workers. The former is more representative of the total population, but for the purposes of a
rough comparison, it is believed that Cantril's data can be used.

> The main community problem is that there is a strong
> party committee which does not allow any other group
> of active people to operate, and it is not possible
> to affect it.
>
> There is no leadership. There is a drug problem. A
> low-level population with little willingness for public
> action. Every activity we tried to organize failed
> because of the institutions.
>
> No communication among the people. Juvenile delin-
> quency. No way for people to meet one another. A
> difficult economic and social situation with a split
> in the local leadership.

The organizational mandate to the community worker, which serves as a powerful determinant of the type of issue selected, also influences the locus of the subcommunity to be organized. This is seen again most clearly in Amidar, where the district manager usually decides which neighborhoods will be singled out for attention. Originally, the "worst" shikunim were selected for organization, i.e., worst from the standpoint of poor upkeep, dirty hallways and courtyards, delinquent rent payments, etc. Because of a singular lack of success, middle-range neighborhoods were then chosen, where conditions had not deteriorated so much with respect to entrances, garbage, and quarrels between neighbors. The primary factor determining the neighborhood-to-be-worked-with was the type of complaint made to Amidar or, from another stand-point, the district director's perception of desired changes in the behavior of the tenants. As one of them expressed his expec-tations of community work: "More cleanliness and fewer problems."

It is not only the presence of certain problematic situa-tions that inspires organization, because there is an intrinsic need for a House Committee in most of the shikunim. Amidar, in its efforts to keep rents low, takes no responsibility for the cost of common utilities, such as electricity for the halls, entrances, and courtyards, and collection of garbage. There is only one meter for electricity in the hallways in most of the shikunim, and tenants are expected to organize themselves and elect someone in whose name the electricity will be registered and who will collect their pro rata shares. Since the electricity is shut off if no payment is received, this serves as a strong incentive to organize. At the same time, most of the tenants have no previous experience with this type of collaboration, and the community worker tries to help them organize for this purpose and, hopefully, use the structure for other neighborhood improve-ment projects.

Similarly, for the Saad workers, the selection of their functional community is influenced by the social service interests of their sponsor in specific population groups. Because the Saad is engaged in the administration of direct services to certain client groups, the community worker generally finds himself trying to improve or develop needed programs for neglected groups such as the aged or youth. It is no accident that the "need" for meals-on-wheels was discovered in 16 communities at about the same time, since this reflected a policy decision within the Saad to provide subsidies in order to promote this particular service, which is highly visible, tangible, and has a strong religious sanction.

The strong identification of the community workers with their organization and its interests was clearly shown in our survey, where less than one-third felt that their sponsor was a hindrance to them, or that the public image of Saad or Amidar interfered with the establishment of relationships to carry out their mission. This is somewhat surprising, since both organizations have a stigma attached to them. The Saad may be identified with the handicapped, the aged, and other nonproductive people who are considered "parasites" in the pioneering ideology of labor Zionism, and the community worker regarded as someone who is connected with relief-giving. Or the community worker may be seen as an arm of the Mayor's office, and either feared or devalued. The Amidar worker may be perceived by most of the clientele and other bureaucrats as representing the landlord and/or the government, but very few of the staff admitted that this was an obstacle to their work. However, in Amidar, where the community workers might have more political maneuverability because their sponsor is external to the municipality and with no official ties or obligations to local government, the staff restrict themselves primarily to the specialized housing interests of Amidar or to social broker roles.

The picture that emerges from the survey is one of good "organization men," most of whom identify with the goals of their sponsor, who regard their mandate as broad, ambiguous but functional, and who perceive their agency as a good or better-than-average place to work. As expressed by one of the community work supervisors:

> In general, I think that we in Israel tend more than
> in other countries to identify strongly with the
> values, goals, and policies of the sponsor because
> we see in them the expression of national values and
> goals. These are very important and unifying factors
> in the light of our situation and our steady on-going
> war for survival.

Since organization theory might lead us to expect more conflict between professionals and the bureaucracies for which they work,[11] how might one account for the evidence of relatively

---

[11] While there is a voluminous literature on this subject, there

little strain between community workers and their sponsors? In addition to the affirmation of mutual interests and shared national values previously noted, there are other possible explanations:

1. While the community workers may regard themselves as professionals, almost all of them are untrained and are subject to rather close supervision by their sponsor. The diversity of their backgrounds, the lack of opportunities for professional education in Israel, and their very recent, somewhat precarious sanction could account for the relatively low order of professionalism. Because the scope and content of community work so closely reflect the specialized interests of its sponsors, it might be more correct to describe the community workers as functional bureaucrats than as professionals, engaged in various forms of <u>neighborhood work</u> and <u>agency-community relations</u> rather than in <u>community development</u>, and seeking administrative involvement rather than substantive participation.[12]

2. Another explanation of the lack of conflict between professional and bureaucratic values is that the community workers have a low threshold of awareness, or are reluctant to express any strong criticism of their sponsor in an interview situation.

---

are relatively few studies dealing with social or community workers, perhaps because their professional status is not always fully legitimated. A definitive paper is W. Richard Scott, "Professionals in Bureaucracies--Areas of Conflict" in Howard M. Vollmer and Donald L. Mills, eds., <u>Professionalization</u> (Englewood Cliffs: Prentice-Hall, Inc., 1966), pp. 265-275. The relationship between social workers and the bureaucracies that employ them is analyzed in Peter M. Blau and W. Richard Scott, <u>Formal Organizations</u> (San Francisco: Chandler Publishing Co., 1962); Andrew Billingsley, "Bureaucratic and Professional Orientation Patterns in Social Casework," <u>Social Service Review</u>, Vol. 38, No. 4 (December 1964), pp. 400-407; and R. Bar-Yosef and E.O. Schild, "Pressures and Defenses in Bureaucratic Roles," <u>The American Journal of Sociology</u>, Vol. 61, No. 6 (May 1966), pp. 665-673.

[12]The distinction between administrative involvement and substantive participation is found in Philip Selznick, <u>TVA and the Grass Roots: A Study in the Sociology of Formal Organization</u> (New York: Harper and Row, 1966), pp. 220-221. The latter concept involves an actual role in policy-making; the former refers to a process in which unorganized citizens are transformed into a reliable instrument for the achievement of administrative goals, under a halo of democracy.

3. A third possibility is that there is little basis for con-
    flict because of the relative absence of constraints.
    Related to the apparently high compatibility of profession
    and sponsor is the very broad, somewhat diffuse mandate
    which the community worker has, giving him, in effect, a
    high degree of freedom of operation in the field. Apart
    from political involvement, there are, as we shall see,
    few restrictions on his activities, and thus he has consid-
    erable autonomy, with little reason to chafe under organiza-
    tional restrictions.

4. Finally, there is considerable congruence between the pro-
    fessional ideology of community development espoused by
    the staff and the values and interests of the sponsors.
    Both sanction only consensual, educational methods, and
    the avoidance of conflict. As a result of the issues se-
    lected and strategies employed, there is a predisposition
    to minimize any possible strain between the sponsor and the
    community work staff.

In this connection, it should be emphasized that virtually
all of the serious problems in Israel, such as inequalities in
income, housing, and education, in addition to the overriding
problems of defense and the economy, are not defined in terms
generally amenable to community work. All of these social conditions are regarded as <u>national</u> problems reserved for action by
the government and the other centralized, politicized bureaucracies, and not by means of local citizen participation. Lacking
the necessary sanction, locus, and resources, community workers
are not expected to have much of an impact on major community
problems. As a result, community work may be useful in getting
a play lot or bus stop and helping tenants deal with problems of
garbage collection (or even establishing a community center, when
funds are available), but they will probably be much less effective in dealing with the more substantial needs and controversial
issues which would involve the city council or the Histadrut.
As one worker put it: "Instead of doing something about the real
needs for better bus transportation and fighting Egged (the bus
company), we instead try to sell language classes."

As local community workers, the Saad and Amidar staffs
are far from the centers of influence on the major systems that
affect their clientele, and they have very weak linkages to the
decision-making structures in housing, education, public welfare,
health, medical care, and employment. Most of these policy and
program decisions are made centrally in Jerusalem or in Tel Aviv
headquarters, and each branch of a ministry in a local community
is, in effect, a field office with relatively little autonomy,
and responsible to its own regional supervisors. Community
workers have few channels of communication to the central offices
of these bureaucracies, and must rely on the very limited

influence they may have on the local staff functionaries, who generally view them as representatives of just another agency.

Community workers are quite sensitive to the charge that they are concerned with "marginal" issues, and justify their choices of problem areas on several somewhat contradictory grounds. It is argued by some that the type of issue chosen is unimportant, since the main purpose of community work is to initiate a socio-therapeutic process which has intrinsic values. Others assert that the issue is just a starting point, a beginning, an entry, or a means to an end, since "one must start where people are." In this sense, the issue might have meaning as a way of moving from simple to more complex problems, from those affecting a small social unit to those affecting a larger one--i.e., from shikun to neighborhood to community-wide problems. Or, it is claimed that the community worker performs an important educational function by heightening awareness and raising questions as a first step toward change. According to this interpretation, community work represents a constructive alternative to apathy and dependence, as well as to hostility and conflict.

These rationales are all part of the ideology of community development, which is professed by most of the staff. In expecting people to progress from simple to more complex issues, however, the normative and descriptive aspects of the process are often confused, since there is no inherent necessity for such a development to take place. Both theory and what little empirical evidence we have suggest that such a process is more the exception than the rule. Studies of community decision-making have shown that different issues require different constituencies, leadership, structures, and strategies.[13] For example, the group that is able to organize itself and keep the hallways clean, or to request meals-on-wheels for older people, may not be the most suitable one to oppose a rent increase or to pressure the Histadrut-sponsored health insurance program for better medical care for older people.

---

[13] Peter H. Rossi, "Community Decision Making," Administrative Science Quarterly, Vol. 1, No. 4 (March 1957), pp. 423-441; Edward C. Banfield, Political Influence (New York: Free Press of Glencoe, 1961); Robert Dahl, Who Governs? (New Haven: Yale University Press, 1961); Roscoe C. Martin et al., Decisions in Syracuse (New York: Anchor Books, Doubleday and Co., 1965), pp. 8-20; Nelson W. Polsby, Community Power and Political Theory (New Haven: Yale University Press, 1963); and Martin Rein and Robert Morris, "Goals, Structures and Strategies for Community Change" in Social Work Practice, 1962 (New York: Columbia University Press, 1962), pp. 127-145.

Even though many of the Amidar workers try to promote the view that the neighborhood and all of its deficiencies (and not just _shikun_ problems) are within the scope of the committee, most of the residents find it difficult to identify with social units larger than their particular floor, entrance, or _shikun_. In part, this may reflect a lack of conviction regarding the benefits of collective action.

Yet, while ostensibly open to a wide range of problems, it is striking how political issues are carefully avoided by almost all of the community workers. Indeed, about one of four staff members stated that they try to stifle discussion of any political issue at their meetings! This is not altogether un-expected, since the sponsors, with their commitment to conflict-avoidance, have in effect instructed the community workers to concern themselves primarily with nonpolitical issues and methods. Because of his location outside the main decision-making structures and channels of the political system, the community worker has only a highly circumscribed ability to mobilize power; therefore, the issues selected will tend to be those that will not require much influence or result in conflict.[14] In view of the highly politicized nature of Israeli society, the avoidance of issues that relate to the party system means that community work removes itself from most of the forces that directly affect the life of its clientele.

Apart from these structural and societal constraints on political issues, the nature of the community development ideology may also explain the sharp divorce between community work and the political system which was revealed in the survey, and acknowl-edged by most informants. For example, among virtually all respondents the survey found invidious attitudes, a basic lack of knowledge, and an extremely low degree of interaction with the local political system and its leadership structure. Almost half of all the community workers did not even know who the political leaders in their community were. Saad workers were even less well informed than Amidar on such matters, and one fourth of the former did not even know if there were political parties active in their area. Furthermore, most of them regarded political parties as "not constructive," and not particularly relevant for their work. These attitudes are, however, not peculiar to com-munity workers, since politics is often identified with the older generation of leaders, and community workers share the negative opinions of many persons under 50 about Israeli politics.

---

[14]This is illustrated in the relative absence of efforts by the Saad community workers to assist client protest against inadequate budgets, and in the reluctance of most Amidar workers to support tenant protest against rent increases in 1966.

The attempt to avoid politics is shown in the following excerpts:

> During election time, members of the committee, many of whom belonged to parties, refused to deal with political business in order not to destroy the faith that the people had in them.

> Political questions came up but I tried to stand off from them. Maybe because of this, I did not try to organize a community council. I feared that it would all blow up because of the possibility of political conflict.

> Before the elections and a month after them, the committee did not meet in order to avoid involving themselves in political questions.

Exceptional are responses such as the following:

> Yes, we consider political questions, and try to find political men. It's worthwhile turning to them so they can help us on issues. Each person agrees to take advantage of his membership in a party in order to help the neighborhood.

The predominance of anti-political attitudes may be a consequence of a professional ideology, which seeks to maximize consensus, harmony, unity of interests, collaboration of diverse groups for the common good, and the denigration of conflict, factionalism, and power struggles--in short, politics is viewed as "dirty business."[15]

Such attitudes contrast sharply with those of the Histadrut, who play the role of political organizers to the hilt, and who are clearly perceived as representatives of a system of power. The Histadrut workers are not at all inhibited in

---

[15] These are among the implicit assumptions of the community development literature, as evidenced in such works as Murray G. Ross (with B.W. Lappin), Community Organization: Theory, Principles, and Practice (2nd ed.; New York: Harper and Row, 1967); Ward Hunt Goodenough, Cooperation in Change (New York: John Wiley and Sons, Inc., 1966); William W. Biddle and Loureide J. Biddle, The Community Development Process (New York: Holt, Rinehart and Winston, Inc., 1965); T.R. Batten, Communities and Their Development (London: Oxford University Press, 1964); Peter Du Sautoy, The Organization of a Community Development Program (London: Oxford University Press, 1962).

attempting to involve people in political processes, and they are not constrained by any notions of professionalism.

Methods, Obstacles, and Outcomes

It has been suggested that the ideology of community development and governmental sponsorship reinforce the lack of sanction for more effective and politicized roles for the community worker, making him more of a functional bureaucrat than an independent professional. There is a circular process at work in which restrictions on methodology shape the range and content of issues, whereby only those issues can be selected which are amenable to the educational techniques open to the professional. The consensual and informational methods employed in community work are, in turn, a consequence of the relatively noncontroversial and marginal issues selected for group action, which largely reflect the interests of the sponsors and the professionals. For example, less than 25 percent and 40 percent of the Saad and Amidar workers, respectively, could recall any project of theirs which was ever strongly opposed by any local political force such as the City Council, a political party, the Histadrut, or another institution. Virtually all of the reported instances of opposition to community work occurred as various forms of internecine conflict. Most of the community workers believe that the other "community caretakers," such as the school principals, Rabbis, mayors, etc., regard them favorably, and are helpful, supportive, or at least show some interest in their work. Eighty percent of the comments made by the respondents in assessing community opinions of their work were favorable.[16] This community acceptance, if it is real, may reflect the restriction of community work to those issues and methods which do not antagonize many people. The cost of this absence of opposition, however, may be a loss of influence on the more important policies and conditions affecting people.

In addition to its sponsors and ideology, community work methods are also shaped by its clientele and the political and bureaucratic systems. In this section we shall describe how the professionals cope with the obstacles presented by (1) the use of political criteria in decision-making, and the related

------

[16]This finding may reflect an inability on the part of most community workers to express any negative feelings about their work, which was noted earlier on pp. 35ff. Some Saad community workers, however, did express the feeling that they were regarded as competitors by the local social workers in the Welfare Department, and that a number of public officials feared or didn't understand their work.

norms and styles of democratic centralism; (2) the low "civic efficacy" of their clientele; and (3) the distinctive bureaupathic attributes of Israeli institutions and agencies with which they must contend.

(1) The use of political criteria in making policy decisions regarding the allocation of social service resources is widespread, and constitutes a challenge to the community worker and his values, since he stands for "objective" welfare standards in the interests of equity and justice. For example, in one community the mayor, who was a member of Mapam (a radical leftist party), opposed the use of the synagogue as a central place to distribute the meals for older persons. In another community, the mayor, who belonged to the National Religious Party, would approve a similar program only for those older persons who attended the synagogue. There are many other reports of interference by members and officials of the political parties and city councils in decisions regarding public assistance and housing, in which they exert pressure to change the rules or to take some action against a family, often for political reasons. Decisions regarding the use and location of meeting rooms and other community facilities are usually entangled with political interests and often decided on ideological grounds. It is not unusual for the Histadrut or a political party to refuse the use of its center, which may be the only one in the neighborhood, for meetings of nonmembers.

In almost every aspect of community life, particularly if he seeks to introduce some change, the community worker finds a political element which has to be reckoned with, neutralized, opposed, supported, or overcome. While most community workers would prefer to avoid politics, it intrudes itself continuously and affects their practice both directly and indirectly. The political character of community life is mentioned repeatedly in the survey. For example:

> My problems are mainly political in trying to bring together people from the different political parties.

> We can't hold meetings in the halls or centers belonging to opposition parties or the Histadrut.

> The major community difficulty is the split that exists between half of the inhabitants who are extremely religious and the other half who are members of the labor party.

> The head of the city council is afraid that pressure groups will be created, so he doesn't want a formal neighborhood council. As long as they're an informal group he'll talk to them.

In dealing with these political forces, the community worker has very little in his background to guide him and almost no support from his sponsor. Furthermore, he has come into the community after the major institutional structures have been crystallized, and is not usually regarded as a legitimate actor in the political game. For example, most of the mayors seem to view the community worker, if they know him at all, as a means of getting some needed social services for aged and youth, and possibly as a source of information about what is happening in the neighborhoods. The relatively few (six) community workers who are assigned to the mayor's office, where they are close to one of the local centers of power, tend to "play it safe," and concern themselves primarily with social service functions and some troubleshooting for the mayor. As one of the community workers observed: "The city likes community work when it keeps the buildings clean, but not when the people begin to ask for services."

One area where the community worker is practically powerless is in confronting the practice of patronage as a basis for filling jobs in the various bureaucracies. This means that many of his colleagues and those whom he may seek to involve in collaboration, coordination, or the modification of a policy obtained their jobs primarily because of party loyalty; thus they are usually not responsive to his call for more objective, "professional" criteria in making decisions. There is also varying recognition of his mandate for community work within the changing vagaries of coalition politics and the recurrent struggle for power over jobs. The community worker is particularly disadvantaged in those towns where crude political patronage and personal favoritism are dominant. In such communities, the staff cannot compete, since they have no access to countervailing incentives and power.

Furthermore, the cultural norms of the form of democratic centralism which characterizes the Israeli political system are at odds with the "grass roots" mode of participation assumed in the community development ideology of the professionals. While there is extensive involvement in elections every four years, the elaborate party machinery is operated by a corps of nationally appointed functionaries, with very little involvement between elections. The pattern of governance in each political party and in the Histadrut consists of a cumulative process of election of delegates who elect other representatives, who in turn elect governing executives, and then a steering or a small central committee which makes the key decisions. Thus authority is successively transferred upwards, further and further from the people who have delegated their consent three and four levels away, eventually to a secretariat which is empowered to act in their name. Once this process has been set in motion, there is really no effective role for the membership except periodically to renew the broad mandate it gives the secretariat. The distinguishing characteristic of this type of decision-making, then, is the transfer of authority from the mass to an elitist leadership, with the result that there is little place for local citizen participation with a direct voice in decisions that affect them.

Another characteristic of this style of decision-making is that leadership is expected to provide an opportunity for the membership to speak out, but it may then act with little attention paid to minority opinion. Once a decision has been made, after an opportunity for expression of different points of view, all members are expected to support it and act in a disciplined way, even though there may be little accountability to a constituency.

This type of participation, which is sanctioned by the dominant public decision-making system, is thus at variance from the one ostensibly promoted by the community workers. Although the vocabularies are similar, the mode of participation which the community worker aims for is much closer to a somewhat idealized American notion of "grass roots," town hall, or participatory democracy, based upon shared, accountable leadership, with widespread direct participation from everyone on all matters affecting them, and the principle of majority rule and protection for minorities. Considerable difficulty is encountered in trying to teach and operate with this brand of participatory democracy. Not only is it contrary to the more prevailing mode in Israel, with which the clientele have some vague familiarity, but it also does not jibe with their own cultural traditions, whether they come from the patriarchal traditional society of the Middle East or the Soviet-type polity found in Rumania or Hungary. The absence of a democratic tradition among most of the immigrants who comprise the clientele of community work is a serious limitation both for their effective use of the political structure in Israel and to the goals of community work. It is to some of these effects that we turn next.

(2) In our survey, the "character of the clientele" was the second most frequently cited obstacle to the practice of community work. The community workers frequently referred to the "inappropriate assignment of people to a shikun," resulting in a preponderance of immigrants from one North African country who, because of their low educational level as well as the dominant influence of the clan, made the task of recruiting leadership and participants exceedingly difficult. Other workers decried their clientele's unfamiliarity with and reluctance to take part in elections to select their representatives to the house or neighborhood committee. Often the community worker is urged to select the representatives, since it is believed that he knows best. In general, the survey revealed a strong tendency in the clientele to be dependent on the community worker, who is often

perceived as a powerful intermediary with the institutions and best qualified to represent them.

These cultural barriers to participation are compounded when the community workers try to involve the more traditional families, or when efforts are made to unite members of different ethnic groups around some common interest. Despite the extent of ethnic stratification in Israel, many of the groups organized by community workers are "mixed." (Amidar professionals report more attempts at inter-ethnic and inter-religious groupings than Saad workers.) There is a wide distribution of the frequency with which inter-ethnic groups meet, with most respondents (particularly Amidar workers) reporting that such activities take place "sometimes or often." Surprisingly, such meetings occur least often in the immigrant towns, where seven of eleven workers reported that attempts to bring together diverse ethnic groups seldom or never take place. Most of these efforts occur in the cities, where the neighborhoods are somewhat less ethnically homogeneous.

When such meetings are convened, what are the results? While 60 percent of the workers report that these meetings are "at least partial successes," their claim should be viewed in the light of the multiple objectives of such efforts, whereby near achievement of any one goal could result in a judgment of "successful." Some typical comments about the experience of bringing different groups together are the following:

> I tried to organize meetings and parties between the Indians and the Moroccans only once. Don't know whether it succeeded because of politeness or because they really wanted to become closer. Both sides are interested but it's done through the committee leadership.

> In the shikun are immigrants from Eastern Europe and from the Middle East. The committee consists of both groups. When they meet, however, the Ashkenazim sit on one side and the Sephardim sit on the other, despite the fact that they have already had numerous activities and projects together.

> Group projects must be separate if people are to be satisfied. A few years ago we tried to organize a seder for various ethnic groups. While they were all together we had to translate into three languages and this detracted from the enjoyment and was very difficult to carry out.

> One of the parents' committees is unable to do anything because the chairman is an educated European

and the others are not. It is full of conflict and
there is no possibility to operate. Actually, this
chairman understands nothing and the others are right.

Yes, the Six-Day War helped. Two blocks of Argentinians
and Moroccans who hated one another before, during
the war sat together and tried to help the heads of
families who were away. Out of this contact they were
ready to help one another.

No, I have really never succeeded in bringing different ethnic groups together. It is one of the
worst problems, and it is the one that challenges
community work the most. The main aim is to create
a committee of active members that also includes the
Ashkenazim. One reason is to prevent the Ashkenazim
from leaving the <u>shikun</u>, because if they do it will
turn into a slum.

The community workers disagreed somewhat on the degree of
difficulties presented by the ethnic composition of their clientele, with the Amidar workers tending to consider it less than
the Saad staff, two-thirds of whom regard it as their major
problem. The following are typical of many replies to the query:
"How would you describe the people you work with?"

Low level. They must be educated toward the Israeli
reality. Our work concentrates on educating them to
participate and accept Israeli values.

North African--low cultural level. We have to use
emotional means, not rational, with them.

Yemenites. It is good that I am also Yemenite and
know their language and they know me.

North Africans--most of them religious. Low average
economic level. The past and tradition influence
them very much; for example, woman's place is in the
home, and if we try to activate her, it causes a conflict between husband and wife.

Mostly Middle Eastern. The lower the level, the
harder it is. They don't always understand what I
want.

Iraq, Yemen, Morocco. They are all poor people.
Their different mentality makes the work difficult.
In the beginning they were very suspicious, although with young people a common language is more
easily acquired.

The project is on a very low level because the people
are apathetic. There is a great gap between youth
and aged. For example, we have classes for illiter-
ates, but they are embarrassed by this and don't show
up. The children feel they know more than the parents
and don't listen to them.

While the community workers as a group did not manifest
any strong prejudice against the Middle Eastern immigrants, a few
described the characteristics of the Moroccans and Iraqis as they
have found them in their experience in rather stereotyped terms:

Moroccans are more spontaneous, more demanding, have
stronger ties with the family. The Iraqis are more
learned, more patient, more cunning.

Moroccans are easily irritated, ask more than they can
give back. Usually they have less education. They
are all backward.

People from Morocco are hot-blooded, but you can win
them by a soft word. People from Iraq are more
enlightened.

Somewhat more thoughtful and less biased comments are these:

Moroccans are patriarchal, frustrated, lack respect
and find it difficult to adjust to reality. A woman's
value is greater the more children she has. Sometimes
they are given to anger. They project their problems
and blame others, not always justifiably. Iraqis are
more unified with themselves unless frustrated.

It is hard to describe Moroccans generally. It depends where they came from, what their background is.
Typical to all, perhaps, is their effervescence.

Each one is different, despite the fact that one can
say that Moroccans are more impulsive and Iraqis more
moderate. They have a different family tradition
which they brought with them.

I think the Moroccan immigration isn't representative
and therefore the public is badly prejudiced about
them. Before they came here they were in conflict
about which values to accept, French or Arab or
Jewish. The tendency was toward the French, but
actually they got only the most superficial aspects
of European culture. In the midst of this process
they came to Israel and, in addition, the bad absorption system of ours destroyed values without

supplying new ones and this caused much of the
problem.

While most other professionals, and indeed the whole
governmental apparatus, including the political parties, Histadrut,
and the Jewish Agency, are concerned with the tasks of absorption
of immigrants and assume socializing functions, many community
workers perceived themselves as the only ones who regard the immigrant population as a client system, and some even view them
as a constituency for whom they take on advocacy roles. Some
workers are clearly overwhelmed with this self-assumed responsibility for all of the unresolved problems and needs of the immigrants. They feel that they are too few in number, and that their
work is comparatively insignificant, "a drop in the bucket." It
is true that relatively few persons are involved in the small
groups organized by the community workers, and perhaps for this
reason there is a tendency, quite characteristic of community
development, to justify the process more in terms of the intangible benefits of participation than specific accomplishments.
Yet, it is precisely because of these cultural obstacles that
community workers perform an important educational function in
helping their clientele learn how to organize and request services.

(3) The character of the clientele--their apathy and
dependency--is, however, a second-order difficulty, at least for
the Saad workers and, to a somewhat lesser extent, for the Amidar
staff. In identifying the major obstacles to community work, the
most frequently mentioned factor was the bureaucratic institutions
with which the workers must deal. Amidar workers cited organizational unresponsiveness, disinterest, and often negative attitudes
toward people, while the Saad staff pointed more to the lack of
sufficient resources, inadequate staff and funds. In general,
the Amidar workers were somewhat more critical of the bureaucracies
and complained of their red tape, inflexibility, lack of communication and coordination, poor judgment, mistakes, and failures
to keep promises. As one worker described it: "The agencies
just don't see the problems of the community. There is no consideration given to the desires of the residents. The agency
knows better--it decides. It built the town; therefore it has
first rights."

The dominant methods for coping with bureaucratic recal-
citrance in all its forms are essentially educational, whereby
the workers try to persuade, inform, and interpret on an individual basis to the staff members of the bureaucracies. The community workers are aware that they have little leverage, but
persist, nevertheless (Amidar staff more than Saad), in trying
to perform social broker roles between their clientele and the
institutional systems. As one of them expressed it: "When I
have problems I never tire of going back many times to the same
people and offices again and again to speak with them about our

work, its positive qualities, the necessity for it, and the importance of answering requests to improve the community."[17]

Another method occasionally utilized by the community workers to deal with the bureaucracies is the development of a group to bring pressure on an agency. Almost as often, however, more or less complete helplessness is expressed: the worker will say that he did nothing because he lacked sufficient knowledge or influence. In dealing with these obstacles, there does not seem to be any difference between the approaches of untrained workers and those with more education and/or experience.

Another approach reported was the attempt to organize an inter-agency committee; Saad workers were almost three times more likely to try this than Amidar. This type of activity was more characteristic of immigrant towns and cities than development towns; somewhat less than half (18 out of 44) of the entire sample reported it. These inter-agency committees are usually composed of other professionals and officials, such as physicians, nurses, sanitation workers, police, Kupat Cholim, social workers, teachers, probation officers, psychologists, municipal officials, and representatives of the Histadrut, Jewish Agency, Amidar, Ministry of Labor, etc. Most of these professionals, together with the representatives of political parties and ideological movements, are agents external to the local community who are dependent on their respective headquarters for financial support and for directions on a day-to-day basis. In addition, many of them do not live in the local community, preferring to commute (particularly in the development towns), and are regarded as out-siders by the inhabitants, who tend to resent them.[18]

Less than one-fifth of the community workers regarded these inter-agency activities as successful, with the Amidar staff over twice as critical of them as the Saad. A typical judgment is "We sat, considered, and not much came out of it. I acted as a mediator." Another is more emphatic: "I don't believe in the usefulness of such a committee. Each service

---

[17]A small number of workers (15), and proportionately twice as many Amidar as Saad, referred to their unmet personal and profes-sional needs or lack of knowledge and skill as constituting their major difficulty: "There's just no one with whom I can share my problems"; "A lack of definition of the job to be done here--where you do everything but actually nothing"; "The work itself hasn't found the right system"; "There is no confidence in the devices that are used; perhaps the system of committees isn't correct."

[18]Report on Urban Development--Implications for Social Welfare, p. 40.

should be dealt with separately. In committees they just chatter."
Another refers to one of the most significant failings: "There
is only ethical or moral authority--that's not enough to bring
changes."

Although there is a legislative mandate for the formation
of coordinating councils, and several demonstration projects have
been attempted, most local efforts to integrate the highly fragmented and politicized social services do not seem to be effective.[19] Lack of communication and coordination among agencies is
a perennial complaint in all countries, but in Israel the conventional obstacles to collaboration have another dimension--namely,
the politicization of inter-organizational relationships in a
highly centralized structure, resulting in a greater-than-usual
strain between the "horizontal" and the "vertical" systems.[20]
As in other countries, national and local priorities and interests
differ. In addition, local needs are highly interrelated, while
the national institutional systems for dealing with them are often
widely differentiated.

An unpublished case study of coordinating councils in
five communities by Leah Shumgar under the auspices of the
Ministry of Social Welfare revealed that the community worker
who took on the staff and convener roles lacked both sanction and
sufficient authority for these functions. The committees, which
were typically composed of representatives of agencies and institutions each of which had a vested interest in maintaining its
own organizational autonomy, lacked clarity as to their mandate
and purpose, and they had little influence. There was also
considerable distrust and fear of the politicians by the social
workers who participated, with the former seeking to utilize the
coordinating committee for political and private purposes, while
the latter strongly resisted any encroachment on their autonomy.
In groping for a way out of a succession of impasses, the committees began to consider broad social problems such as the

---

[19]There are at least three types of local coordinating structures in Israel: (1) the Vaadot Saad, a Welfare Advisory Committee; (2) Marcaz Kehilati, a Community Council, primarily in the
development towns; (3) Vaadot Kehilati, a Coordinating Committee
similar to a council of social agencies. In addition, there are
numerous ad hoc, functional coordinating committees concerned with
the aged or the prevention of juvenile delinquency, but their
effectiveness appears to be quite limited.

[20]The horizontal system is locality-based while the vertical
system is external to the local community, according to the usage
of Roland L. Warren, The Community in America (Chicago: Rand
McNally and Co., 1963).

absorption of newcomers, reducing the proportion of people leaving the community, and other large issues over which they had little or no control. The more they deviated from their initial goals of concrete action to coordinate services, the more they appeared as a potential threat to the city council, which began to put additional obstacles in their way. While admittedly a limited study of only five communities during 1963-65, there is considerable impressionistic evidence to support the generalizations regarding the failures of local attempts at inter-organizational coordination.[21]

A related obstacle to the practice of community work which inheres in the bureaucratic structure is found in the Histadrut, which was usually among the first institutions transplanted to the new towns and settlements. Consequently, most of the opposition which the community workers face is in the form of either bureaucratic resistance or internecine conflict, often with the Histadrut for the same constituency.

For almost ten years the Ministry of Social Welfare and Amidar regarded the field of urban community work as their domain, and had established a rather informal geographical division of labor, but this seems to have become somewhat less workable in the light of the broader conception of Amidar functions promoted during the last few years. (Similarly, Saad and Amidar workers do not always recognize the validity of a division of functions between them, and many of them do not see any difference between the goals of their respective organizations.[22] This is seldom problematic, however, since they are found together in only six communities.)

Toward the end of 1967 the Histadrut assigned at least 45 staff members to devote more intensive efforts to selected neighborhoods where perhaps 60 percent of the population belonged to the Histadrut. This was regarded as a new organizational effort, supplementary to and intensifying the ongoing cultural and educational programs and the ordinary membership maintenance activities,

---

[21] An example of a demonstration project that seeks to overcome the usual local obstacles to inter-agency coordination is "Proposal for a Social Planning Service in Or-yehuba," by Ephraim Eliezri and Meyer Schwartz, Jerusalem, August 7, 1969 [restricted communication]. The project will be sponsored by the United Nations Office of Technical Cooperation and the Directors-General of the Government of Israel.

[22] One-third of the Saad and 60 percent of the Amidar workers surveyed did not recognize any differences between their two organizations.

all of which were carried out by a staff who were appointed to
their jobs on the basis of party affiliation and service. The
Histadrut staff were not regarded as legitimate community workers
by the Saad and Amidar staff, who viewed them as interloping
competitors and representatives of an authoritarian political
institution seeking to extend its hegemony over all aspects of
community life. They were correct in that the Histadrut functions
as a political and economic power structure, and as such can compete very effectively with Saad and Amidar community workers, who
are constrained by their professional and organizational values
and interests from getting involved in political struggles.

The Histadrut often seeks to organize neighborhood committees on a political basis, whereby persons are elected in
proportion to the strength of their party in the national elections. This is in contrast to the heighborhood committees
sponsored by Saad and Amidar, which are open to everyone on a
nonpartisan basis. The Histadrut has challenged the representa-
tiveness of organizations sponsored by Saad and Amidar and has
accused them of being self-selected groups, in contrast to the
presumably more democratic character of the Histadrut-sponsored
organizations. On the other hand, some Saad and Amidar workers
have claimed that the Histadrut, instead of trying to organize
new or competing parallel committees, has tried to take over
groups that they have organized, or take credit for others'
achievements. In general, the Histadrut is seen by most community
workers as concerned only with the maintenance of its own power,
as not really interested in the "little things" that affect
people, and as a major obstacle to change.

The Histadrut workers, as noted earlier, do not regard
themselves as "professionals," but rather as members of a cadre
carrying out an organizational mission. Their general attitude
is that the leaders know the needs of the people best and what
should be done, as is evident from some of the following quota-
tions:

> We have to help structure an attitude. We guide the
> people so that they will be able to determine for
> themselves, but we direct them to reach decisions
> which are good for them.

> The worker should know exactly what he wants and he
> should guide the people.

> We have to train cadres of active members from the
> neighborhood and to structure it culturally.

They believe that people view them in a favorable light as representatives of one of the major institutions that has influence in
the country:

> A referral by the Histadrut is advantageous. People
> know that you can apply to the Histadrut with just
> anything--a personal or a community problem.

They have no hesitation in working with political officials and
in making use of their contacts with various institutions. In
contrast to the feeling of competition which Saad and Amidar
workers often expressed toward them, the Histadrut workers claim
that they cooperate; they do not feel that they are in competition,
but they believe that they have considerably more power and influence in their work with the same constituencies.

How do the community workers cope with the pressures ex-
erted by the sponsor, the clientele, and the political, bureaucratic system? How do these factors affect their style and professional role? The fact that the staff members tend to identify the
community problem or "need" more or less unilaterally and in line
with the sponsor's mandate and interest may now appear to be quite
"functional." This practice may be necessary in view of the limitations of their clientele. As perceived by the staff, the clients
lack the capabilities for full participation in a democratic, cooperative process of problem definition because of the absence of
a tradition of citizen participation, a low stake in the community,
traditionalism, and ethnic and cultural differences. Furthermore,
the issues have to be restricted to those for which the community
worker has suitable and sufficient sanction and resources. Many
basic needs of the clientele have to be excluded because the community worker is outside the political structure, lacks power,
and is reluctant to use methods involving conflict.

Accordingly, once he decides what the issue will be, the
community worker organizes an ad hoc group of the most capable
or active persons he knows; or if there is an existing committee,
he brings the issue to them for action. In the latter case, he
does not usually rely upon the committee to "discover" needs by
themselves; he takes the initiative to assert the need for a
project, and then tries to secure their approval. This process
is described in the following excerpts:

> I go from house to house to see if there is a need
> for the project at all. Afterwards I speak with
> members of the committee. Sometimes I distribute
> questionnaires and it comes to the committee for
> consideration.

> In the beginning I took those who were willing to
> deal with the problems in the community because in
> time they will become known. I try usually directly
> to bring up problems that the committee should con-
> sider. I suggest the topic and if they accept it
> we take care of it together.

Many work alone in these early stages and do not seem encumbered
by organizational structure; as one worker put it: "Afterwards
I invite the committee, involve them, and they do the rest."
Thus by selecting the most resourceful persons, they see that
the job gets done.

> I conduct a survey and discover that I should begin
> with these projects [a center for the aged]. I
> invite those who are capable, explain the purpose,
> attempt to get volunteers. I choose those most fit
> for the job. I set up committees according to the
> problems that arise and pick appropriate people for
> the job. I try to encourage a particular person
> even if he is not the most popular if I feel that
> he fits the job at hand.

> I try to interest them in a project and train them
> to carry it out. I bring up the problems at the
> committee meetings and they decide what to do.
> Sometimes I help in carrying it out. When I think
> they can tackle it alone, I stay out of it.

The propensity of the clientele to delegate responsibility
is dealt with in different ways by the Saad and Amidar workers,
with the former much more likely to approach other agencies on
a professional-to-professional basis rather than through a
citizens' committee. The majority (25) of the two groups combined
claim to use either method ("depending on the situation"), but
over three times as great a proportion of Amidar workers say that
they _always_ work with and through a committee. The use of committees is also favored more by the more experienced and/or
educated worker.

A strong commitment to predetermined goals was evident
in the responses to some hypothetical situations designed to
elucidate professional ideology. Respondents were asked with
reference to the recent projects they had described whether it
was better if the community worker knew precisely what he wanted
to achieve or if he should try to help the people decide what
they wanted to do. Only one Saad worker opted in favor of the
latter, while three-fourths of his colleagues chose the former
and five gave a qualified response of "It depends." Typical of
the community worker's designation of goals is the following:

> I wanted to start a youth center, and I made the
> people conscious of the fact that it was vital for
> the youth. If I had been more indirect and had not
> pushed as hard, it would have taken another year.

Opposed to this view is the belief that "the worker should know that he works with people and should know that their aims come first." In almost none of the responses was there any recognition of a possible conflict in goals between the community worker and his clientele.

In general, then, one gets the impression that the community worker, like his sponsor, knows what is good for "them," and uses his energies to mobilize support for these goals. It may be that the lack of continuing participation of which the workers frequently complain is due to this rather paternalistic mode of operation. This pattern is probably found in its most extreme form among the Histadrut staff, which, on a continuum of unilateral to directive actions, are at one end, with the Saad and Amidar workers somewhere near the center. However, the difference may be only that the Histadrut workers are more self-consciously directive, while in actual practice the Saad and Amidar workers function in much the same way, even though it is not consistent with their ideology. Thus, the differences between them might be more of degree than of kind, with the Histadrut articulating the partisan goals and purposes of a political and social movement, while the Saad and Amidar workers stress the self-determination and self-help values of community development.

While most of the community workers deal with the limitations of their mandate, locus, methodology, and resources by functioning more as bureaucrats than as professionals, by concentrating on a narrow range of somewhat specialized, marginal issues which are of particular interest to their sponsors, and serving as social brokers, there are a few examples of practice which reveal possibilities for various forms of social action. The ideology of community development and the Israeli community decision-making system is evidently sufficiently flexible to permit staff members with political capabilities and a strong commitment to social change to select more controversial issues around which to organize, and to utilize methods which will bring them into conflict with the established institutions. Despite the fact that most of the workers claim they are prevented from organizing citizens against the government, since with a monopoly on community work it is their only possible employer, some staff members who recognize that government is not monolithic have mobilized pressure against the schools, the mayor, the local social welfare bureau, and the city council. A few community workers have even used their political acumen in the rather dangerous game of trying to play off one political party against another, or, similarly, to take advantage of the continual strain between the Histadrut and local government to get support and funds from one or the other for a particular program. Others have demonstrated the possibility of developing new, independent citizens' associations on a community-wide basis around a common problem, such as the needs of the aging, and of broadening the scope of concern from block to neighborhood to community.

The superior strength of the professional commitment and capabilities over organizational and structural limitations is particularly evident in Jerusalem, which constitutes a "deviant" and possibly test case of the opportunities for community work under what might appear to be most adverse circumstances. Formerly concerned mainly with the administration of neighborhood centers, the Department of Group and Community Work is part of the municipal social welfare bureau, a notoriously bureaucratic agency whose administration of public assistance has been the subject of several investigations, and whose policies and practices are in poor repute both in the professional social welfare community and the government. In addition to what appears to be an inhospitable organizational environment, community work was for many years strongly opposed by the deputy mayor who had the social welfare portfolio in the Jerusalem City Council. Furthermore, Jerusalem is a highly stratified, traditionalist city with a large concentration of orthodox neighborhoods. Yet when one compares the community work programs in the two other largest cities, Haifa and Tel Aviv, where this function is also a department of the municipal social welfare office and subject to only negligible control and supervision from the Ministry of Social Welfare, but where it enjoys in many ways what appears to be a highly favorable organizational and community environment, one notes that it is in Jerusalem that broad forms of citizen participation have been developed.

In Jerusalem community workers have sought to play advocate roles, to convert a clientele into a constituency, and to focus on social action as well as social services. For example, eight neighborhood-based committees were federated in a combined attack on the problems of the aging. (Staff assistance had been given earlier to stimulate citizen action to force the city to provide medical care for some 2600 aged persons who were suddenly declared ineligible for services because of a transfer in the auspices of 12 clinics.) Strong threats, demonstrations, and eventually bargaining with the mayor and members of the Kenesset resolved the issue. The Municipal Department of Education has also been the target of citizen action, aided by community workers, to protest the quality of education provided for children of Middle Eastern families. Pressures have been put on the Department of Education by both groups of parents and a small number of community influentials, with the staff utilizing both mass and elite strategies of social action. Community workers have also been concerned with the changing policies and practices regarding dropouts and juvenile delinquents, and have acted to force more "integrated" school classrooms.

These activities are quite atypical. Much more characteristic is the restriction of community work to much less controversial and social service-focused issues, on the needs of individuals or families organized in small groups on a neighbor-hood rather than on a community basis.

Chapter III

CONCLUSIONS

Summary of Findings

Urban community work, a relatively new program in Israel, is under the auspices of two governmental bureaucracies--the Ministries of Social Welfare and Housing. Its recent sanction, its somewhat ambiguous quality, its ancillary function in each department, and its very limited staff resources--all contribute to its relatively low status and power both on the national level and in the 35 local communities where it is sponsored as a professional service.

Four operating goals are found in the practice of urban community work: (1) to stimulate the development of needed social programs and to improve the delivery of existing services; (2) to improve social relations among different ethnic groups and encourage citizen participation; (3) to educate new immigrants to accept certain Israeli values and norms; (4) to convene local agencies to facilitate better communication and coordination. In carrying out its mission, the character, issues, and methods of community work tend to be shaped primarily by the short-term, tangible organizational interests of its governmental sponsors, which are congruent with the ideology and capabilities of the staff, rather than by the more long-range planning and integration goals of community development.

The community worker functions mainly as an arm of the public welfare system in implementing some of its program development objectives, or as an agent of Amidar with its concern for property management. A minority of the Amidar staff have a broader conception of their goals than their administrators, but almost all of the community workers, in contrast to other types of professionals, seem to identify with and support their bureaucratic sponsor and the establishment of which they are a part. While they regard themselves as independent professionals, they perceive few if any conflicts between their goals, those of the state, their auspices, and the needs of their clients. The newness of community work and the lack of a common educational background among the workers contribute to its precarious professional status. Because of these factors and their agency-community relations duties, the community workers might more accurately be conceived as "functional bureaucrats" than as professionals. Their primary aim may be to seek administrative involvement rather than substantive participation.

CONCLUSIONS

In the local communities, small numbers of persons are involved episodically, usually in ad hoc groups, in attempts to secure amenities such as community centers, recreational areas, improved housing maintenance, and social service delivery. In this way, community work helps bring about minor service improvements and environmental modifications. It also serves as a vehicle for adult socialization, and is in fact more of a force for social control and system maintenance than social change. Because of its emphasis on work with individuals and groups, community work in Israel has more in common with certain types of settlement-sponsored neighborhood organization or group work in the United States than with community development.

In addition to nurturing some forms of neighborhood organization, information and referral services, and the administration of direct services to groups, some community workers also promote case committees and other efforts at inter-agency coordination. These are usually not regarded as successful because of the lack of sanction and suitable authority necessary for interorganizational work in a highly centralized and politicized system. Even when community work is located in the office of a strong and supportive mayor, where it might have fairly broad possibilities for action because of its linkages to the political system, there is a tendency to utilize the opportunity primarily for administrative and direct service functions, along with residual and trouble-shooting tasks for the mayor.

In view of the highly politicized nature of Israeli life, the lack of relationships between community work and the political structure is striking. The major social problems of Israel are defined in national terms and are usually not suitable for local community work. In addition, avoidance of political involvement is nurtured by the ideology of community development, with its emphasis on consensus and a harmony of interests, in contrast to the struggle for power and ideological conflict characteristic of Israeli politics. The staff commitment to this philosophy, together with the specialized interests of the sponsors of community work, probably account for the somewhat marginal character of the issues selected for citizen participation and the limited influence of the staff. Located outside the dominant public decision-making systems, the community worker often lacks the appropriate resources for influencing the politicized, centralized bureaucracies that control the jobs, housing, medical care, education, and assistance needed by his clientele. In addition, he may also have to defend his claim to organize this constituency in the face of competition from other institutions such as the Histadrut.

The professional ideology is, however, quite elastic, and with a different emphasis, commitment, and capabilities, a few community workers have demonstrated the possibilities of social action by organizing groups on a community-wide basis around a common social problem. In general, however, the community work values of localism, participatory democracy, and an apolitical style strain against a paternalistic type of democratic centralism in which political criteria prevail over professional values. Although community workers profess the enabler role model, and often function as social brokers and adult educators, most of them seem to act in an assertive, unilateral manner as they pursue predetermined goals, selecting appropriate action systems and issues. Yet there appears to be relatively little continuity, increased collaborative competence, or the development of indigenous leadership, perhaps because so much of community work seems to be project-centered.

The community workers report that their major obstacles are the rigidities and inefficiencies of the various social service bureaucracies, and the apathetic and dependent character of the former immigrants who comprise their clientele. Because of the absence of a tradition of voluntarism and democratic participation, the socializing function of community work takes on considerable importance, since it represents one of the means of making some of the new citizens aware of their rights and opportunities as they learn how to request needed services. However, only meager success has been achieved in helping the different ethnic groups collaborate on a sustaining basis.

The constraints of the cultural barriers to participation, the professional ideology, the locus and status of community work within centralized, politicized bureaucracies, and the interests of its two governmental sponsors appear to limit significantly the efforts to develop autonomous, self-help groups that can change their living conditions and increase their social competence.

The Future of Community Work in Israel

Under these circumstances, then, what are some of the future possibilities for community work in Israel? Five alternatives were identified among community workers, governmental officials, and social scientists:

1. There are some who say that it is either too late or too soon for community work to be any different. Perhaps it might have been able to play a more significant role in the early sixties, immediately after the Wadi Salib riots, if additional resources had been made available. Now the number of workers is too small, and most of them lack professional training. It is possible that community work might have a more substantial impact within the next decade if it can expand, become more professionalized, develop more confidence in its mission

and capabilities, and be sponsored by various nongovernmental organizations.

2. Others, particularly some of the social scientists, argue against continuing support of community work and assert that it is hopelessly "foreign" to Israeli society in its belief in local citizen participation as a means of change. Consequently, it is a waste of resources, and its perpetuation is an illusion if not a hoax.

3. Others, however, see it as a useful instrument for all governmental bureaucracies who might employ community workers to serve as social brokers between themselves and their clientele. This is essentially an expansion of the present major purpose of community work found in Amidar, except that the Ministries of Health, Education, Labor, and Absorption would all be implementing their own community relations policies.

4. From another perspective, community work is seen largely as a social planning function on the local, regional, and national level, sponsored by the government but involving other institutions such as the Histadrut and the political parties.

5. Finally, a more politicized version of community work is advocated whereby community work would enter the public decision-making arena, establish formal and informal working relationships with political parties and the Histadrut (or work against them if need be), and also try to develop independent citizen associations.

In evaluating these alternatives, primary attention will be given to the last two. The third is essentially a projection of the present conception of community work to other bureaucracies, which would try to organize somewhat the same constituency; hence, the analysis which has been developed regarding Saad and Amidar would also apply to them.

Any judgments regarding the future of community work in Israel will be influenced by (1) an assessment of present political and social trends in Israel and (2) a conception of the goals of community work and its capabilities.

(1) The degree to which certain socio-political trends emerge will determine the possibilities of community work, and in this sense they constitute pre-conditions for a promising future for such work.

(A) One of the most critical elements determining the degree to which locality-based interest groups are feasible and can be effective is the likelihood of more power residing

in the local community and the enhanced ability of people
to identify with it. This may come about through the evolution of a more open, responsive political system, which
would be evidenced by a smaller number of parties, a lessening of emphasis on ideology, and possibly a slight increase in the authority of local communities. It is assumed
that if the political system becomes more democratic and
less paternalistic, more directly responsible to the wishes
of the citizens through such measures as the direct election
of mayors, then the development of interest and pressure
groups outside the political party structure would be more
feasible.[1] These new organizations would function as
secondary, voluntary associations, standing between the
citizen and the power of the government, the parties, and
the Histadrut. There will probably be more desire and
opportunity for the expansion of voluntary citizen participation as more Israeli citizens become middle class, educated, and politically sophisticated. It would not be
unlikely for voluntary groups to emerge in Israel, where
they would at least be permitted to function, although
their influence might be quite limited. All of this
depends, of course, on the nature of the military situation
confronting Israel, and its ability to maintain politics-
as-usual.

(B) With the passage of time, it can be expected that the
representatives of the Afro-Asian immigration will have
more influence on the local and ultimately the national
party machinery.[2] The mobility prospects for these immigrants are greater in the political structure than in
other areas of the society, but it is not possible to
predict to what extent they will be co-opted or narrow the
gap between the "Two Israels." It is almost certain that
they will persist in their relatively disadvantaged position, and will continue to require greater access to the
governmental bureaucracies, the political parties, and the
Histadrut to obtain better education, housing, medical
care, and employment opportunities. While community work
is certainly no substitute for comprehensive national
programs aimed at eliminating relative deprivation and

---

[1]Some evidence for the decline of politics and ideology is
cited in Dorothy Willner, "Politics and Change in Israel: The
Case of Land Settlement," Human Organization, Vol. 24, No. 1
(Spring 1965), pp. 65-72, and Fein, p. 224.

[2]See correspondence from Shlomo Avineri, Commentary, Vol. 45,
No. 4 (April 1968), p. 21; see also Weiss, "Local Government in
Israel."

increasing social mobility, there will be a continuing need for some forms of social brokerage, advocacy, and community development in the development towns and low-income neighborhoods in the cities if they are to avoid the fate of residual communities with a concentration of poor people who are excluded from the mainstream. Yet, community work as presently sanctioned, structured, and supported appears to have little capability for either playing a more effective political role or becoming a more assertive social broker for its clientele. The Saad and Amidar staffs are small in number, and their mandate and locus too limited for a large scope of operation. As a relatively new program operating outside the dominant decision-making system, with low status and power and no long-range plans for strengthening or expansion, community work will probably maintain its present character, becoming more institutionalized and bureaucratized within this structure, and maintaining its resemblance to group work and agency-community relations rather than to community development.

(C) Under somewhat different circumstances with additional sponsors, however, it is possible to conceive of community work which could help people move into participation in the political and other established structures, as well as create some new local, regional, and national organizations for citizen action which could serve as pressure and interest groups. Comprising a "third force," these nonpartisan, citizen associations could be organized around residence, functional, or ethnic interests, and be concerned with social service issues such as education, medical care, housing, recreation, and employment. They could try to get the bureaucracies to improve, extend, and expand their services and benefits and, in addition, bring pressures on the political parties who might even compete for their support. It should be recognized, however, that these forms of social action, by pitting "haves" against "have-nots," recent immigrants against veteran settlers, might be a highly divisive force, further straining the fragile social fabric comprised of East and West, and religious and non-religious groups. From this perspective, perhaps community work should remain nonpolitical. On the other hand, if there are grievances and inequities, it might be more desirable to provide for some institutionalized expressions of collective action than to ignore or suppress these problems, even though there is always the possibility of increasing frustration because community work would be unable to exert sufficient influence on the resource and decision-making systems.

(2) The extent to which community work has a role to play in accelerating or facilitating any loosening of the political

structure, and/or in providing the needed technical assistance for the community development, social brokerage, and advocacy needed by low-income groups, depends in large part on the degree to which its social service or social action capabilities are stressed. This is largely a function of its sponsorship.

If community work is to become influential and be a force for social integration and change, it will proably have to become more political, or at least not be limited to noncontroversial issues and collaborative and educational methods. It is because Israeli society solves its problems through the conflict of the political process that the community worker as a bridge or harmonizer is quite limited. Since the social service bureaucracies have political power and respond to pressures, the community worker may have to get into the struggle if he wants to influence them. While the issues would probably still be mainly social service-centered, the methods and strategies could be more varied and include more overt forms of pressure, or at least mild coercion, negotiation, bargaining, and perhaps even conflict tactics. Since it is highly questionable whether such methods and strategies can be promoted under governmental auspices,[3] different sponsors who could sanction and tolerate more diverse and assertive forms of community work, as well as specially qualified staff, would be required. At the very least, then, one of the prerequisites for a different future for community work is the possibility of some alternate nongovernmental sponsors who would permit the use of a wider range of issues and methods. Where are they to be found? New sponsors of community work might come from among the following: ethnic, civic, and fraternal associations, organizations of former immigrants, voluntary social service agencies, the universities and their four schools of social work, and a new consortium in the form of an Israel Community Development Fund, which could sponsor a series of demonstration projects. Other groups which might be organized for civic action are the growing number of middle class, voluntary, community service clubs and associations whose energies could be mobilized for both local and national projects. These sponsors might provide staff services for their own organizations, as well as for selected groups not presently sought out by the Ministry of Social Welfare, Housing, or the Histadrut. Each type of sponsor could promote different forms of community work; for example, social planning might be promoted as part of a demonstration project or by the Ministry of Interior. The schools of social work would have rather wide latitude in developing educational programs, and could jointly create a training

---

[3] Ralph M. Kramer, _Participation of the Poor: Comparative Community Case Studies in the War on Poverty_ (Englewood Cliffs: Prentice-Hall, Inc., 1969), pp. 262-265.

center which would send its students to staff a broad range of
groups in the community.

These forms of locality-based citizen action constitute
only one part of what should be a two-pronged effort; the other
consists of the strengthening of the <u>social planning</u> function.
The major thrust of local social planning up to now has been the
attempt to coordinate services, but this has suffered from a
lack of appropriate authority on the local level as well as a
lack of sanction for the convener. Less emphasis on formal
coordinating councils and more on ad hoc groups focused on single
social problems might be one way of dealing with the distribution
of power in Israel, on the assumption that few permanent structures would have the authority and the responsiveness required.
While it is not likely that the structural sources of the lack
of coordination can be easily modified without greater delegation
of autonomy and decentralization of functions, some countervailing
power might be developed through the institution of a social
planning function in the office of the mayor subsidized by the
Ministry of Interior or Absorption. Such a staff person could
give professional leadership in identifying local needs and resources, and in drawing up plans and priorities with citizens
and other agencies and groups.[4] It might be more feasible to
attach such a social planning consultant on the regional level
and provide for some inter-community planning. In either case,
for this social planning function to be reasonably effective,
some clear, vertical channels to the national government would
have to be provided.

It would be presumptuous to specify the details of a
social planning structure for Israel without much more study.
All that can be said at this point is that social planning is a
neglected aspect of community work whose scope should include
the participation of the affected clientele, interested citizens,
as well as the official agencies and institutions of the government and the polity that is Israel.

All this has implications for the education of different
types of community workers, particularly with respect to the
social planning function. The worker fulfilling this latter
function could be described as a "technipol," i.e., one who has
the technical skills to design feasible plans and programs for
different types of population groups, and the political capabilities to implement them. Such a person might also make a contribution in introducing the social dimension in physical and
economic planning on the national level. For these purposes,
a new type of professional will have to be educated by the

---

[4]See Chapter 2, footnote 21 for an illustration of such a
proposal.

universities and their schools of social work: one who is not merely an agent or functionary, but one who can help shape policy goals, who has a sense of professional identity and a social philosophy, and who is accountable to a constituency and a profession and not just his sponsor.

The potential for urban community work in Israel, then, lies in the possibilities for greater diversity in sponsors and modes of practice, so that it will not be confined primarily to governmentally sponsored work with neighborhood and functional groups, but will also include some forms of social planning and community action under a variety of auspices.

COMMUNITY DEVELOPMENT IN THE NETHERLANDS

Chapter IV

INTRODUCTION

Most descriptions of Holland begin by noting that it is
the most densely populated country in the world: almost 13
million people living in an area one-quarter the size of New
York State or approximately half of San Bernardino County,
California. Equally distinctive is the remarkable continuity in
the political and social development of Holland, with its three-
hundred-year-old tradition of nationhood culminating in a stable
and effective democratic government. This achievement is particularly notable because of the deep cleavages of religion and
social class that have historically divided the population into
a series of isolated and self-contained groupings.[1]

Originating in the late sixteenth century, the Dutch
nation developed into a highly decentralized republic led by a
burgher elite until about the middle of the nineteenth century,
when a constitutional monarchy was established with a strong
central authority. At that time, Holland was a rather stagnant,
agrarian, small nation of about three million inhabitants; but
in the last century, it has increased its population by 400 percent and its net per capita income by 250 percent as a result
of industrialization and modernization. These vast social
changes have been accompanied by the increasing centralization,
bureaucratization, urbanization, and democratization of Dutch
life.

Today, with less than 10 percent of the population engaged in agriculture, and with a high standard of living, Holland
can be characterized as a post-industrial society. It is a predominantly middle class, advanced, welfare democracy. It is
highly stable, with an astonishing degree of satisfaction registered by its citizens with the shape of their society. Many
years ago John de Witt, one of the foremost leaders of the Dutch

---

[1]The paradox of a stable and integrated yet highly stratified
society is perceptively analyzed in Arend Lijphart, The Politics
of Accommodation: Pluralism and Democracy in The Netherlands
(Berkeley: University of California Press, 1968) and Johan
Goudsblom, Dutch Society (New York: Random House, 1967). The
latter volume is the primary source of much of the basic information in the discussion below unless otherwise indicated.

republic, aptly expressed one of the dominant motifs of his
country when he declared: "The interest . . . of this State [is]
posed in this--that calmness and peace be everywhere and that
commerce may be carried on unhindered."[2]

The high degree of national unity and stability is the
product of a unique pattern of religious stratification and
pluralism, in which the dynamic interaction of Calvinists, more
moderate Protestants, and Roman Catholics has shaped the character
of both the polity and the society. It has led to a modus vivendi
among these religious groups of live and let live which contrasts
sharply with the recurrent upheavals in other countries. In
part, these accommodations have been sustained by the geographical
distribution of the Christian denominations, whereby Catholics
tend to be concentrated in the south and the more rural regions,
and the Protestants in the northern and more urbanized parts of
the country. According to the census in 1960, the population
was approximately 40 percent Roman Catholic, 28 percent Dutch
Reformed (Protestant), 9 percent Calvinist, and 19 percent "unaffiliated" (which includes some small Protestant sects).

These religious groups exist within a pattern which has
been characterized as "segmented integration," an outcome of the
unique Dutch phenomenon of _verzuiling_.[3] This concept, usually
translated as "pillarization," provides the basic key to the
understanding of Dutch society. Just as Zionism or the "in-
gathering of exiles" is the dominant motif in the State of Israel,
so the process of _verzuiling_ is the principal theme that illumi-
nates the major forces shaping the practice of community work in
Holland. _Verzuiling_ refers to the idea that "the various blocs
of the population represent separate pillars (_zuilen_), each
valuable in its own right and together indispensable in supporting the national structure."[4] Each of the three largest denominational blocs--Roman Catholic, neo-Calvinist, Liberal Protestant--

---

[2]Quoted in Hans Daalder, "The Netherlands: Opposition in a
Segmented Society," in Robert Dahl, ed., _Political Opposition in
Western Democracies_ (New Haven: Yale University Press, 1966),
p. 193. Daalder's essay is a definitive analysis of the Dutch
political system.

[3]The effects of _verzuiling_ on the social institutions of Holland
are cogently discussed in Goudsblom, pp. 50-57 and 71-127. Cf.
David O. Moberg, "Social Differentiation in The Netherlands,"
Social Forces, Vol. 29, No. 4 (May 1961), pp. 331-337, and
Lijphart, pp. 16-58.

[4]Goudsblom, p. 32. The principle of _verzuiling_ was used by the
government in planning for an appropriate mix of the various
religious and "unchurched" groups in the new towns of Holland.

together with Humanists and other secular groups has established an array of organizations encompassing practically every sphere of social and political life, including separate schools and universities, political parties, trade unions, employer associations, health and welfare agencies, sports and leisure time associations, newspapers, and radio and television stations. For this reason, Holland has been described as neither a pluralistic nor a mass society but rather as "a 'communal society,' characterized by strong intermediate groups that are <u>inclusive</u> in the sense that . . . the closely interconnected set of organizations in each bloc encompass all aspects of their members' lives."[5]

The educational system, for example, as one of the most powerful social influences, clearly reflects the "vertical pluralism"[6] characteristic of Dutch society. Before 1900 almost 70 percent of the Dutch children attended government-sponsored public schools. Today the proportions are reversed, and most children attend schools sponsored by one or another of the religious denominations. These have been subsidized by the government since 1917, which sets only minimum standards regarding administration, curriculum, degrees, number of teachers, and teacher qualifications. Approximately one-third of all families send their children to Roman Catholic schools, 30 percent to Protestant schools, and 40 percent to "neutral" public schools. In this way, the schools tend to perpetuate <u>verzuiling</u> and the social isolation caused by a sectarian education. The influence of the religious blocs over the lives of their adherents is reinforced by the high proportion of membership in their political parties, sports and radio associations, and unions, to which over one-half of all adults belong. For these reasons it has been said:

> A Dutchman can live an isolated life within a
> homogeneous ideological environment from the
> cradle to the grave, meeting people of different
> outlook only in the street, the army, and perhaps
> in the factory or office and more recently on
> television screens.[7]

---

[5]Lijphart, p. 179. See also William Petersen, "Fertility Trends and Population Policy: Some Comments on the Van Heek-Hofstee Debate," <u>Sociologia Neerlandica</u>, Vol. III, No. II (1966), pp. 2-13.

[6]The term "vertical pluralism" to describe <u>verzuiling</u> is found in Moberg, "Religion and Society in The Netherlands and in America," <u>American Quarterly</u>, Vol. 13, No. 2, Pt. 1 (Summer 1961), pp. 172-178. Goudsblom uses the concept of "segmented integration" to refer to the same social condition.

[7]Daalder, p. 214. Two representative empirical studies of the degree of religious involvement and some of the consequences of

Not all of the _zuilen_ are based upon religion, since there is another set of secular or organized socio-economic interest groups in the form of the liberal and Socialist parties who, because of their world view, also claim the total allegiance of their members:

> In principle both liberals and Socialists reject
> _verzuiling_; yet in practice they have had to accept
> it and assume themselves the role of _zuilen_ in the
> shifting coalitions with the two [Roman Catholic
> and Orthodox Protestant] confessional blocs.[8]

The relationship between these two blocs (secular and religious) is complicated because the orthodox Calvinists and Roman Catholics launched a successful emancipation movement in the latter part of the nineteenth century--decades before the working class responded to the call of socialism. As previously noted, the religious blocs obtained state support for their schools in 1917, ending a fifty-year struggle and institutionalizing the practice of governmental subsidies for all social services under religious auspices.

The _verzuiling_ process is changing as it comes under increasing criticism in the face of pleas for more ecumenicity and the pressures of a modernizing society.[9] There is disagreement as to the extent of "de-pillarization" (_ontzuiling_) in Holland, although there is impressionistic evidence that an increasingly large proportion of the population is unaffiliated with the various _zuilen_. It has been estimated that perhaps over one-fifth of the population in the urban areas is "unchurched," and that this proportion has increased to over one-half among intellectuals, professionals, and industrial workers. Trends toward de-pillarization persist despite the continuation of the government's policy of distributing all subsidies on a proportional

---

verzuiling are: J. Weima, "Authoritarianism, Religious Conservatism and Socio-Centered Attitudes in Roman Catholic Groups," _Human Relations_, Vol. 18, No. 3 (August 1965), pp. 231-239, and I. Gadourek _et al._, "Involvement in Cultural Systems in The Netherlands: Its Measurement and Social Correlates," _Social Forces_, Vol. 40, No. 4 (May 1962), pp. 302-308.

[8]Goudsblom, p. 125.

[9]Informative presentations of some current attitudes are found in _Delta_, Vol. 9, No. 4 (Winter 1966-67): Otto J. DeJong, "Dutch Protestantism," pp. 5-16; Daniel DeLange, "Dutch Catholicism," pp. 17-30; and Henk Schaafsma, "Mirror of a Pillarized Society: Broadcasting in The Netherlands," pp. 57-59.

basis to the various organizations of the religious subcultures, and carefully balancing all governmental advisory bodies with representatives from each. Although the confessional blocs are still the dominant power structures outside the largest cities, many social scientists believe that _verzuiling_ has reached its peak. The process of de-pillarization seems strongest in the towns and in the upper middle class; it is least strong in the lower middle class and in the countryside. Religion, in general, seems to be a variable that increases in importance as community size decreases and areas become more rural. In the towns and cities, religious affiliation seems to be less and less signifi- cant in obtaining employment, and in the last three or four years voters have been crossing party lines and reading newspapers of the other _zuilen_. De-pillarization seems to be a much less con- troversial issue since the process has been set in motion; it may be primarily a matter of the rate of change. Secularization and inter-bloc cooperation are proceeding more rapidly in some fields of social service than in others; in this way the Dutch pattern is becoming more like the American, where sponsorship may be restricted to members of one religious group, but the service is available to the community.

Yet the alignments and the shifting secessions and coali- tions between the religious institutions and the socio-economic blocs still constitute the great dividing lines in Holland, and are not only reflected in the educational, leisure time, and social welfare systems, but are also an intrinsic part of the unique political structure.

The Political System

Formally a constitutional monarchy, the Dutch State, like Israel, is a unitary one, with the central government possessing a higher degree of authority than most federal structures. The scope of government has grown over the years, and there is a high degree of national regulation and social legislation in the government, which is a union of authoritarian and democratic principles with free elections based on the principle of propor- tional representation. While some allowance is made for decen- tralized authority, all major taxes are collected by the national government in The Hague, and in every important field of activity, policy is determined nationally. For example, the municipalities have little voice in police matters because the local force is responsible directly or indirectly to the Ministry of Domestic Affairs in The Hague.

The pattern of local government is quite complex, and is significant for the practice of community work because of the distance of the political system from popular control. In con- trast to the United States, municipal government is based on the

principle of collegial administration with divided executive
authority.[10] Three elements are involved in Dutch municipal
government: (1) a council (Raad) elected for a four-year term,
which functions as a watchdog rather than as an initiator of
action; (2) an executive function divided between the Mayor
(Burgemeester), who is appointed by the Crown, and (3) the College
of Wethouders, composed of two to six members of the council who
are elected by the council, and who usually reflect its party
composition. Once elected by the council, the Wethouders together
with the Burgemeester constitute a cabinet or municipal executive
committee and are often referred to as the Gemeente (the municipality), just as the cabinet in parliamentary practice is termed
the "government." The College functions as an executive committee and carries day-to-day responsibility for the management of
municipal affairs, allocating among its members the various
administrative functions in a manner somewhat similar to commis-
sion government in the United States or to the local councils in
Israel. The Council has the final authority on policy matters,
but in actual practice the municipal government is really domi-
nated by the College, and particularly in the smaller communities
this means that the Burgemeester is the central political power.

There are over 950 municipalities in Holland, many of
which have fewer than 1,000 inhabitants, and while there is recognition in The Hague of the need for regional government and
consolidation of marginal local units, this process proceeds very
slowly. While there is an old tradition of planned and cooperative endeavors in the creation of the largely man-made environment
in Holland, along with the centralization of governmental powers,
there are also strong feelings of local autonomy and resentment
of outside authorities and their attempts to influence the community. This lack of cooperation among smaller communities with
common interests serves, as we shall see, as one of the rationales
for community work. However, in carrying out their mandate, community workers must cope with another distinctive attribute of
the socio-political structure in Holland--namely, the very limited
popular participation and general lack of interest in political
and community work. Numerous studies have confirmed the existence of considerable apathy and lack of knowledge among the
citizens in a political system in which there is little direct
popular control.[11] Only the local and provincial legislatures

---

[10]The description of municipal government presented here is
based on Robert L. Morlan, "Cabinet Government at the Municipal
Level in the Dutch Experience," _Western Political Quarterly_, Vol.
17, No. 2 (June 1964), pp. 317-324.

[11]Daalder, pp. 189-190. Daalder and Robert C. Bone, "The
Dynamics of Dutch Politics," _Journal of Politics_, Vol. XXIV, No.

and the house of the national legislature are elected directly
by the people. Elections take place less than once a year, and
though voters are fined for not appearing at the polling station,
they are not forced to vote. Approximately 95 percent participate
in the elections.

An example of the relationship between citizens and their
local government is the following:

> Attendance by private citizens at Council meetings in
> the average city is a rarity, even when controversial
> topics are at hand. The Hollander seems definitely
> committed to the principle of representative govern-
> ment, and is taken aback at any question as to why no
> one attends the meetings. His response is likely to
> be: "Why, those matters are for the Council to de-
> cide. I'm in no position to judge. . . . That's
> what we elected them for. If we don't like what they
> do, we'll work it over next election."[12]

The concept of a "participant culture" is thus missing in the
civic life of Holland, and there is no strong tradition of citizen
interest groups outside the religio-political power structure
that might exert pressure or intervene in the process of community
decision-making. The Dutch civic culture has been characterized
in this manner:

> On the basis of cross-national comparisons one can
> safely conclude that the Dutch are relatively passive
> even when faced with the possibility of grave polit-
> ical injustice or injury. They are also reluctant to
> take overt action as individuals. But when they do
> act, they usually resort to a collective effort, often
> through an already existing organization. These
> tendencies--especially the relatively low degree of
> activism and the relatively high reliance on estab-
> lished associations--lend strong support to the con-
> tention that the Dutch are highly deferential in their
> political attitudes.[13]

---

1 (February 1962), pp. 23-49, and Lijphart, pp. 139-180, are the
primary sources of the generalizations about the Dutch political
system in this discussion.

[12]Morlan, p. 24. Current developments among the Dutch political parties are discussed in A. Hoogerwerf, "Latent Socio-political Issues in The Netherlands," Sociologia Neerlandica, II (1965),
pp. 161-179.

[13]Lijphart, p. 154. The concepts of participant culture and
civic culture are derived from Gabriel A. Almond and Sidney Verba,

Hans Daalder speaks of the "mixture of both deference and indifference which has tended to characterize the attitude of most
Dutchmen toward authority."[14] There is thus a high degree of
congruence between the social and the political structure: both
are elitist and sustain deferential patterns of authority which
do not appear to be conducive to preparation for active roles
as citizen participants. Although there are many signs of an
increasing interest in social action, a high degree of satisfaction with their circumstances is still expressed by most
Hollanders, and there is a corresponding lack of vision of how
life might be different. To many outsiders, Holland presents
the self-image of a "finished society" with very few social problems to be solved.

Yet Holland, like all other countries undergoing rapid
change, has had to face some of the inevitable costs of industrialization and urbanization: overcrowding, overpopulation,
housing shortages, traffic congestion, air pollution, etc. There
is also structural unemployment, excessive migration to the urban
areas stemming from the declining agricultural economy in certain
regions, the transformation of villages into towns as a result of
the establishment of industry--with consequent tensions between
oldtimers and newcomers, and the steady deterioration of older
working class neighborhoods in the larger cities. An increasingly large part of the population now live in modern town and
city developments set up according to officially planned and
rather uniform designs, usually on the perimeter of the established urban areas.[15] Living in high-rise cooperative apartments,
many of which are owned by the various _zuilen_, the inhabitants
tend, like most suburban dwellers, to be young families drawn
from all over the country, but with very little community and/or
religious identification. The distribution of these housing
developments, as well as their rental policies, has the effect
of reinforcing the socio-economic stratification in Dutch society,
resulting in considerable homogeneity within each of a series of
enclaves.

These, then, are some of the major characteristics of
the socio-political context within which community work functions

---

_The Civic Culture: Political Attitudes and Democracy in Five
Nations_ (Boston: Little, Brown and Company, 1965).

[14]Daalder, p. 197.

[15]A thoughtful analysis of some of the distinctive Dutch
problems of urbanization is to be found in Peter Hall, "A
Polycentric Metropolis: Randstad Holland," _Delta_, Vol. 10, Nos.
1-2 (Spring-Summer 1967), pp. 5-32.

in Holland. Before the organizational structure and major settings for this practice are described, some terminological matters
will be discussed and the historical background for the current
uses of community work in Holland briefly sketched.

A Note on Terminology

> This concept [community organization] from the English-
> speaking world appeals to us.[16]

It is instructive that at the European Meeting of Community Development Trainers convened by the Ministry of Cultural
Affairs, Recreation and Social Welfare of The Netherlands in
November 1967, there was agreement to avoid the use of the term
"community development and substitute "a broader and more neutral
term, 'community work'," on the grounds that use of the latter
might "prevent many futile discussions on definitions of concepts."[17] Community work was taken to include: (1) community
development, focusing mainly on self-help and in the rural areas;
(2) community organization, focusing primarily on inter-organizational exchange, coordination, and planning; (3) community education; and (4) the community aspects of public administration,
city and regional planning, adult education, youth services,
public health, mental health, social welfare, housing management,
urban development, cooperatives, home economics, and rural extension.

In view of the extensive scope of activities included
under these rubrics, it is not evident to what extent this usage
constitutes a long-needed clarification. Untangling the terminological confusions in the Dutch literature on community work is
a formidable task in itself, and is made even more complicated
by the lack of suitable translations for various concepts which
are not free of ambiguity in Dutch, whose referents are not
clear, and which cannot always be distinguished from each other.[18]

------

[16]Dr. G. Hendriks, Community Organization: A Collection of
Readings on Social Planning and Community Organization (The Hague:
Ministry for Social Work, 1964), p. 17.

[17]European Meeting of Community Development Trainers (Report
on a meeting of experts under the auspices of the Dutch Ministry
of Cultural Affairs, Recreation and Social Welfare at Dalfsen,
November 5-9, 1967), p. 15. This terminology is also discussed
in W.A.C. Zwanikken, "The Netherlands Institute of Community Development," Community Development Journal, No. 6 (April 1967),
pp. 51-55.

[18]There are at least three major terms used in Dutch to refer

Part of the obfuscation stems from the frequent use of the terms "community development" and "community organization" interchangeably, with each conceived as program, method, philosophy, or movement. Often, community organization is conceived as a method employed in the process of community development, which in turn is conceived as synonymous with all forms of "social development," including various types of inter-organizational work, adult education, and social guidance, as well as direct work with population groups to induce them to take a greater interest in their problems and make themselves responsible for finding solutions.

One consequence of this lack of conceptual rigor is that in Holland the ideology of community development, with its connotations of self-help and participatory democracy by means of grass-roots citizens organizations, is often used to refer to social planning or, more specifically, inter-organizational work seeking to coordinate various social welfare agencies by means of a federated structure.[19] For example, in some of the governmental publications, public or citizen participation is usually considered synonymous with the process of involving delegates from the pillarized social welfare structures in the community. One of the results of this blurring of distinctions between community development and social planning is the failure to distinguish between a "functional" or social work community, and a geographic community, as well as the significant differences between elitist and mass patterns of community decision-

---

to community work: maatschappelijke opbouw, samenlevingsopbouw, and opbouwwerk--all of which literally imply "upbuilding," but are used to denote social development or community organization. These concepts are discussed in Nos. 1, 2, and 4 of the NIMO Bulletin, published during 1967. See in particular the article by J.J.G.M. Vroemen, "Het Werken aan de Samenleving: Verkenning van een Terrein," NIMO Bulletin, No. 1 (January 1967), pp. 12-19 and the discussion on pp. 6-8, NIMO Bulletin, No. 4 (November 1967). A definitive analysis of the development of community work is Bram Peper, "Afbraak van het Opbouwwerk? Een Beleids-sociologische Kritiek," Mens en Maatschappij, V. 44, No. 2 (March/April 1969), pp. 113-134.

[19]For the distinction between community development and social planning which is used as the basis of this analysis, see Kramer and Specht, Readings in Community Organization Practice, pp. 10-11. For a different perspective on these concepts which stresses their interrelatedness, see David Popenoe, "Community Development and Community Planning," Journal of the American Institute of Planners, Vol. 23, No. 4 (July 1967), pp. 259-265.

making, and between representative and participatory democracy.[20]

Actually, the use of the term "community work" can be helpful in differentiating three subtypes which are found in Holland: (1) inter-organizational work, which is more appropriately considered an aspect of social planning and which, as was noted, is often called community development; (2) direct services to groups usually described in Dutch as buurtwerk, which is a rather flexible and responsive form of leisure-time programming by neighborhood centers in which the agency's constituency is regarded as broader than the actual or participating membership, and where the agency seeks to serve the needs of the entire geographic area in which it is located; (3) authentic forms of community development utilizing "initiative groups" or grass-roots, neighborhood groups. There may be a semantic gain if the term "community development" is restricted to (3), which is the focus of this study, even though its practice in Holland is much more limited than the other two forms of community work.

Historical Background

Current community work in Holland has a twofold root: in the pillarized organizational structure of social work, and in a series of social planning efforts--mainly in the depressed, more rural parts of the country.

Before World War II, social work was not a primary concern of the confessional blocs, and the various forms of public assistance, psychiatric social work, child welfare, probation, etc., were sponsored by local governments or private organizations not affiliated with religious groups. During the war, however, when most of the men were deported as slave laborers, many of the churches organized home-help services and, later, family welfare agencies to provide material assistance and practical help to families. After the war, the churches expanded these programs, partly for political reasons and partly as a response to what was seen as the declining role of religion in modern society. It was widely believed that sponsorship of social work services would be a means of strengthening the various denominations. The churches in Holland sought to become

---

[20]See G. Hendriks, Social Planning and Community Development (The Hague: Ministry of Cultural Affairs, Recreation and Social Welfare, 1967), pp. 23-32. On the importance of the distinction between the functional and the geographic community, see Murray G. Ross, Community Organization: Theory, Principles and Practice (2nd ed.; New York: Harper & Row, 1967), pp. 41-44.

somewhat more like their counterparts in the United States; they
tried to change their image by becoming more involved in various
community and family problems. Social work training was expanded,
reflecting the pattern of casework and group work education as
they emerged in the 1940's in the United States.

In the postwar period, in almost every town and rural
area in Holland, separate social work agencies in all fields of
service were organized by Roman Catholic, Orthodox and Liberal
Protestant, and Humanist groups, each of which had parallel
counterparts on the provincial and national levels. This development was facilitated by the subsidy policies of the Dutch government, which eventually provided for up to 80 percent of the costs
of general social work, services for families and the mentally
deficient, homemaker services, and group work. In addition,
subsidies were made available for the coordination of social
work, and within each of the zuilen, separate coordinating bodies
were formed for each of the various fields of service on the
local, provincial, and national levels. The role of the government was seen as coordinating, stimulating, and subsidizing,
rather than as the direct provider of services.[21]

By the 1960's, however, there was increasing dissatisfaction in governmental circles regarding the duplication, overlap-
ping, and fragmented pattern of services, which involved many
submarginal units in the uncoordinated services sponsored by the
various zuilen. In the newer communities, the zuilen structure
of social work had little relationship to the new inhabitants,
and it was unable to meet the changing needs in many of the
smaller towns and rural areas. Newer forms of social work had
developed which did not fit in with the preexisting confessional
structure, such as community development, buurtwerk, social
rehabilitation, and work with multi-problem families. Because
the local and provincial welfare councils contained only representatives of the zuilen, the government decided in 1965 that
coordination could only be subsidized if a new and broadly based
structure to coordinate governmental and voluntary agencies was

---

[21]A summary of the principal subsidy regulations in the field
of social work can be found in the Digest of the Kingdom of The
Netherlands: Social Aspects (Netherlands Government Information
Service, n.d.), pp. 82-86, and in "Government Regulations on the
Subsidies for Private Bodies in the Field of Social Welfare,"
Ministry for Social Work, 1962. The subsidy regulations pertain-
ing to community work are summarized in NIMO Bulletin, No. 4
(November 1967), pp. 1-4. One of the prerequisites for govern-
mental subsidy of staff costs is the completion of a one-year
training program currently offered at the Rotterdam School of
Social Work.

developed, in which other interests besides those of the sponsors would be represented. New planning councils on the local, regional, and provincial levels were authorized for government subsidy, and during the last few years, these bodies have gradually been organized as local consultative and advisory agencies in the field of social welfare. In the process, however, community development in the form of direct work with population groups has been given little emphasis. It has been anticipated that neighborhood centers and adult educational programs would assume primary responsibility for this type of activity.

A second source of interest in community work originated in various efforts during the 1950's to stimulate the social and cultural development of those areas where economic and physical planning did not produce the expected results. These were regions characterized by a rural exodus and /or structural unemployment. Government funds were made available for the construction of neighborhood and community centers, swimming pools, libraries, gymnasia, and sports fields, along with subsidies for certain forms of group work that would involve the population. In the new housing estates, in the depressed rural regions designated as "stimulation areas," and in the deteriorating sections of older cities, the aim was "to direct the groups of a population to new aims, to increase participation of groups and individuals and specific development projects, to change people's attitudes. . . ."[22]

In 1957 a Dutch translation of Murray Ross's textbook (see footnote 20) provided much of the theoretical justification for community work in Holland--as well as in other parts of the world. The movement grew (along with a community "self-survey" movement) and was marked next by the publication of a Dutch text

---

[22] Willem A.C. Zwanikken, _Community Development in The Netherlands: NIMO_ (The Hague, 1967), p. 2. NIMO (The Netherlands Institute for Community Development) was founded in 1966, and has given professional leadership to the development of community work both in Holland and elsewhere in Europe. It is the sponsor for the European International Clearing House for Community Development and is the source of much of the information provided here on the development of community work in Holland.

The economically underdeveloped and depressed rural areas known as "stimulation areas" and their problems are discussed in Hendriks, _Community Organization,_ pp. 57-66; H.J.H. Boderie, "Special Social Policy in the Dutch Stimulation Areas" (The Hague: Ministry of Cultural Affairs, Recreation and Social Welfare, 1965); and Jacob E. Reinders, "The Netherlands Development Areas Reach a New Phase," _Community Development Journal,_ No. 5 (January 1967), pp. 26-29.

on community organization (<u>Maatschappelijk Opbouwwerk</u>) by Miss J. Boer, long-time executive of the Drenthe Provincial Development Council, in 1960. Perhaps best known are the prolific writings of Dr. G. Hendriks, who later became the Deputy for Social Development in the new Ministry of Cultural Affairs, Recreation and Social Welfare in 1965, and who has an international reputation as one of the foremost ideologues of community development.[23]

By 1967, subsidies were available for seven types of community work in seven different organizational settings, for eight kinds of community facilities and amenities, and for training in community development. Altogether these national subsidies totalled 44 million guilder in 1969 (over ten million dollars), with at least 20 percent more in the form of local matching funds.

Community Settings and Organizational Sponsors

Four different community settings with a distinctive role for community development have been identified:[24] (1) rural areas in which there has been agrarian reform, or which are underdeveloped socially and economically, or which have been selected for industrial development--and where the traditional ways of life are altering and there is a need to promote good relationships between long-time residents and newcomers, as well as to create new sociocultural amenities; (2) small towns which have experienced rapid growth through industrial expansion, requiring new organizational structures to involve the population in planning new services; (3) old urban neighborhoods in need of rehabilitation or conservation to improve both housing and the sociocultural infrastructure; and (4) newly created urban neighborhoods which need to be made more livable and which are characterized by little or no identification by the new residents with the community.

These different types of communities or geographical areas require different types of community work with distinctive goals, methods, structures, and resources. For example, in the urban neighborhood there may be <u>buurtwerk</u> or community development which stresses community education much more than social action or change. On the city, regional, or provincial level, one will probably find more community activity in the form of interorganizational work stressing coordination. Finally, there are

---

[23]Some of Dr. Hendriks' major writings have been collected in the two publications cited in footnotes 16 and 20.

[24]Hendriks, <u>Social Planning and Community Development</u>, p. 19.

structures for social planning at the national level: the National Council for Social Welfare (Nationale Raad voor Maatschappelijk Welzijn) and the Ministry for Cultural Affairs, Recreation and Social Welfare ("CRM").

Sponsors of Community Work

The organizational structure of community work in Holland is extraordinarily complex, as can be seen from the following brief descriptions of six major types of sponsors. While all are regarded as "private," they are wholly subsidized by various levels of government, with most of the government resources invested in efforts to promote inter-organizational coordination rather than to stimulate resident participation on the locality level.

(1) Provincial Development Councils (Provinciale Opbouworganen).

These councils are found in each of the eleven provinces and have a board of directors composed of representatives from the leading social work, religious, professional, and civic organizations. Their task is mainly to coordinate and stimulate the development of social welfare in its broadest sense. Including local governmental officials, the provincial, regional, and city-wide councils are supposed to advise various governmental bodies in matters of social and cultural welfare. The definition of the scope of social welfare may vary from the relatively narrow concept of social work to a much broader concept of physical planning and economic development, which expresses the view of some CRM social planners, but which is rarely used as a working definition. Most of the provincial development councils have initiated community development projects, especially in areas where there are insufficient social, cultural, and recreational facilities--or in communities where major social changes are occurring. Each provincial council employs one or two community workers who are often assigned to one of the regional councils [see (2) below].

(2) Regional Development Councils (Regionale Welzijnsstichtingen).

These councils, or welfare foundations, include representatives of the major religious, social, and professional sectors. They are usually found in the rural areas, and work among clusters of small villages. They may employ a community worker themselves, but typically they receive staff service from a provincial development council. There were at least 20 regional development councils in Holland and another three in an early organizational stage as of 1968.

(3) Urban Development Councils (Stedelijke Opbouworganen).

After 1965, urban development councils were initiated in
cities with more than 75,000 population, with the same structure
and functions of the provincial councils--namely, to bring
together social welfare agencies to stimulate cooperation and
facilitate communication. Much of their attention is given to
new areas in and around urban cores, in which the population
often increases to 50,000 people over a period of three to
five years. It is believed that these new areas need community
development to stimulate self-help and to initiate the establishment of new facilities. In addition, urban development
councils are concerned with the older areas in the cities which
have deteriorated and which lack modern facilities. There were
11 urban development councils in Holland in 1968 among a total
of 42 "macro" community work agencies on the provincial, regional, and city-wide levels.[25]

(4) City, Area, or Neighborhood Development Councils
    (Wijkopbowourganen).

These are usually organized by urban development councils
or local governments with the customary representation from
agencies, and they function in the areas regarded as problematic. There are 13 neighborhood development councils involving
eight community workers; many of the projects are only one or
two years old.

(5) Neighborhood Centers (Buurthuizen).

These agencies are the most frequent sponsors of what could
be considered community development in Holland, and are found
in both rural and urban areas. They date back to the first
part of the twentieth century, when the neighborhood centers
originally had group work, adult education, and youth-serving
functions. In the last ten years, some of them have begun to
take some responsibility for community work in their neighborhoods, in addition to their traditional direct services to
groups. There are more than 525 such neighborhood centers,
settlement houses, and group work agencies, together with
village centers and other special urban projects. There are
95 subsidized community development projects in Holland on
this locality or "micro" level.

(6) Functional Community Organization (Functioneel Opbouwwerk).

This is a specialized form of practice which has as its
goal the greater community involvement of the various religious

---

[25]Zwanikken, <u>NIMO</u>, p. 5. This does not include over 325 community and village centers, mostly without trained staff, some of
which were established through a community development process.

groupings in the community. A limited amount of functional work is sponsored by the various _zuilen_, but much of it is not regarded as authentic community work by many of the professionals.

While community development in Holland can be classified according to these six sponsors, and further subdivided according to whether the community is small or large, rural or urban, the units of action are all very small in scale, i.e., small-sized neighborhoods and collections of villages.

At the present time the major goals for community work in Holland seem to be the maximization of the values of social welfare rationality and modernization by means of citizen participation. The social planning objective is assigned to a complex, hierarchical structure which seeks to coordinate a multiplicity of denominationally sponsored (but governmentally subsidized) agencies, in an effort to achieve greater coherence, efficiency, and effectiveness. This organizational structure is considered the principal means for stimulating collaboration among the representatives of the various confessional blocs. Serving as a centripetal force in a highly fragmented social service system, social planning is expected to compensate for some of the more dysfunctional aspects of subsidy policies and practices by bringing more order into and better control over the management of the social welfare enterprise.

This attempt at what is largely inter-agency housekeeping is seen as part of a process of "democratizing society" through the promotion of citizen participation, which in turn is often regarded as an end in itself and an antidote to the growing complexity, institutionalization, and bureaucratization of Dutch society. As stated at a recent conference of community work sponsored by The Netherlands Institute of Community Development (NIMO): "The central function of community work in every dimension is dynamizing and democratizing the community against the rigid tendencies in society."[26] Thus citizen participation serves a twofold purpose: it is a vehicle for accomplishing certain _tasks_, such as inter-agency coordination and modernization, and, as a socio-therapeutic _process_, it strengthens the forces of participatory democracy in a highly stratified society.

---

[26]In connection with this political objective of community work, the City Planner of Amsterdam was recently quoted in an interview: "There is a lot of discussion about democratization of government and local authorities, but they never speak about democratization of economic power concentrations and pressure groups. Private initiative is nothing compared to economic power concentrations" (_NIMO Bulletin_, No. 2 [April 1968], p. 12; translation by T. Hijna).

INTRODUCTION

Survey Methodology

It is against this background and organizational structure
that we shall review the findings of an exploratory survey of the
practice of community work in Holland during the summer of 1968.
The data are derived from interviews with 46 community workers,
all of whom were engaged full-time in the practice of community
development in the sense in which we have defined it, i.e., direct
work with affected population groups. In addition, 15 other governmental officials, social scientists, and other experts were
interviewed. All but ten of the 46 staff respondents were interviewed in Dutch by two sociology graduate students and an experienced neighborhood center executive with both a social work and
a sociology background, who also functioned as a research assistant. The interviewing and translations were supervised by Dr.
Henrik van den Berg of the Vrije Universiteit of Amsterdam, who
also served as a research consultant. The questionnaire was
basically similar to the one used in Israel, although it was somewhat shorter, more structured, and required an interview of about
an hour and a half.

The names of the 46 respondents were drawn from a list of
150 community workers of all types prepared by The Netherlands
Institute of Community Development. It is believed that the
sample represents at least 80 percent of all those defined by
NIMO and other knowledgeable persons as engaged in community
development in Holland.

The 46 respondents were in 36 different communities, including 22 urban areas and 14 rural communities. The urban areas
included the five largest cities. Forty-two different agencies
were represented, including 17 neighborhood centers, 12 regional
development councils, and 13 other welfare foundations. Thus,
over 60 percent of the sample included what can be described as
micro-community sponsorship and practice in neighborhood centers
and the rural areas. In addition, three functional community workers were interviewed: a Roman Catholic, a Dutch Reformed, and a
Liberal Protestant--all on the village or neighborhood level.

It should again be noted that the focus of this inquiry
was not on inter-organizational work, which is often designated
as community development in Holland and which is more appropriately regarded as a form of social planning, but rather on the
practice of a selected sample of staff members who are mainly
involved with efforts to mobilize citizens to induce them to
take a greater interest in their problems and to make themselves
more responsible for solving such problems in the urban neighborhoods and in the more rural regions of the country.

We shall first analyze the staff members' perceptions of
community problems and needs, and their professional response to

these recognized conditions, i.e., the issues and projects selected for more or less systematic attention, the methods used
to achieve goals, characteristic outcomes, and some of the leading internal and external variables influencing the practice of
community work.

Chapter V

ANALYSIS OF SURVEY FINDINGS

The Most Important Community Problems

In the more urbanized areas, the most important community problems perceived by the respondents were: (1) the lack of public recreational and cultural facilities, social amenities, and social services (typically, the workers identified as "community problems" those recreational needs on which they happened to be working at the time); (2) the character of the population-- its "apathy," as well as the existence of social distances between old and new residents, between middle and working classes, and between the residents and their unresponsive local government; and (3) the physical condition of the community, usually the deterioration in housing.

In the more rural areas, where the regional development councils are found, the most frequently cited community problems were (1) economic, stemming mainly from a declining agricultural base, which has led to the emigration of younger persons, (2) inadequate facilities, (3) traditionalism in village life (such as the "backwardness" manifested in the prevalence of religious orthodoxy), (4) lack of local leadership, and (5) a high degree of provincialism, whereby villages compete with each other and insist on separate facilities. While the impact of economic forces was fairly well recognized in the rural areas, there was somewhat less awareness of the effects of industrialization in the more urbanized areas--e.g., population shifts which had led to the development of new communities on the perimeter of these areas. Common to all settings, however, was the importance attached to the lack of public facilities and the problems arising from the population's lack of interest in solving community problems.

Four typical illustrations of community problem perception are summarized below:

N, an isolated neighborhood of 4,000 inhabitants with a poor reputation, is cut by two railroad lines and a large park. The housing is old and overcrowded, and the area is used as a "reservation" for antisocial families who cannot find housing in other parts of the city. There are many impoverished families, high unemployment, and numerous physically and mentally

handicapped people. There is a dearth of citizen
interest and leadership, as well as a lack of space
for recreational and cultural facilities, inadequate
community services, and little cooperation among
social agencies in the area. For example, there is
a casework agency which serves 50 problem families,
but does nothing else. Another group work agency
maintains a clubhouse for youth, but has no contacts
with other agencies. Efforts to organize a development council have been unsuccessful.

Many outsiders have come to live in T, but they are
not made to feel at home, and a strain has developed
between them and the original inhabitants. The town
council has ignored them, as well as most requests
to improve social and cultural life. There are no
playgrounds, and there is water pollution, but year
after year nothing is done about these matters. Although there is full employment, there are no theaters,
concert halls, or other cultural facilities. The
municipality wants to do everything by itself and
does not consider the wishes of other towns in the
vicinity.

There are major economic, social, and cultural deficiencies in this town in the southern part of Holland.
There has been very little economic development in
the area, since most of the people worked in the
mines not far from the town. There has always been a
lack of facilities for recreation, education, youth
work, the aged, and social work in general. When the
mines closed, a serious problem of unemployment developed which made the lack of services and facilities
even more acute. The development of more adequate
services is hindered by the lack of cooperation among
the different villages and conflicts among the local
organizations.

Young people are migrating and aren't willing to work
in A. They don't see a happy future for themselves
in industrial work, and they don't see any social
provisions. These attitudes have traditionally made
people emigrate to Canada. Now they are going to the
Randstad, but the more highly industrialized cities
just don't attract them.

It is noteworthy that the respondents rarely mentioned
several community problems that were singled out as serious by
the various social scientists and national officials who were
interviewed. These include the special economic, social, housing,
and medical needs of the aged (particularly in the large cities),

juvenile delinquency, and other manifestations of intergenerational problems.

These and other problem-conditions may be obscured by the vast number of separate agencies operating in a field of service. For example, there are almost 30 different agencies concerned with the aged in Amsterdam, although none have the capability of dealing with the needs of at least 25 percent of the older persons who are living there under extremely poor conditions. In one province, there are over 100 different social work agencies; most have only a single staff member, but this sustains an "illusion of service."

Apart from the fact that the needs of certain groups get lost in the complexities of the inter-agency network, there are two other possible explanations for the selective perception of community problems by the professionals, and their response to them. In Holland, as in most other countries, the major problems pertaining to the economy and housing are defined nationally because plans and policies are formulated at the national level. Community workers in a locality are therefore not expected to be able to deal with larger issues such as structural unemployment or a housing shortage. While a few professionals may recognize the existence of these more serious problem conditions, the mandate, locus, resources, and methods of community work are usually not appropriate or adequate to cope with them.

Another social-psychological force operating to restrict the scope and content of community conditions recognized as problematic is the previously mentioned widespread tendency to believe that there are relatively few serious domestic problems remaining to be solved in Holland. The image of an almost finished society is widespread, and is reflected in the high degree of satisfaction with the current state of affairs registered in Dutch public opinion polls. For example, the existence of poverty in Holland is not generally acknowledged, but a recent study sponsored by the Ministry of Cultural Affairs, Recreation, and Social Welfare revealed that one-seventh of the employed persons could be classified as "deprived" on an economic and social participation scale. This report was never released, since it would have embarrassed the government. The Socialist Party, however, made a similar study on its own, and finding somewhat the same conditions, gave widespread publicity to the findings over its own television network early in 1968.

Issues, Projects, and Methods Found in Community Work Practice

Despite the different organizational structures and settings for community work, their rural or urban character, and the socio-economic status of the population, there is a great similarity in the types of "recent characteristic projects" reported by the staff members. The three most frequently cited examples were (1) the creation of an organizational structure for community problem-solving, which usually took one of two forms: (a) the organization of citizen "initiative groups," usually as a means of carrying out a survey of recreation and cultural needs as a preliminary to the establishment of some facility or service, or (b) the organization of some type of council structure for inter-organizational exchange; (2) the establishment of a playground, swimming pool, sports field, library, community center, or a summer program for children; and (3) the provision of direct services, usually recreation and leisure-time programs, typically sponsored by neighborhood centers.

Illustrative of the many projects reported were these:

An organized group of residents and agency representatives supported a proposal developed by a priest and youth worker to convert a piece of land which had been unused for many years into a playground. Initially, the local government did not even respond to two letters from these groups requesting a change in land use and technical and financial assistance in establishing a playground. When the City Council eventually rejected the request, the local residents who were on the committee became discouraged and dropped out. Several professionals and the community worker continued to press the matter and ultimately succeeded in persuading the local government to change its mind and approve the establishment of a playground. Once this occurred, the residents rejoined the committee and were involved in further development of the plans.

A group of parents in a new neighborhood in Amsterdam began to collect signatures for a petition to the municipal government to build a swimming pool. They argued that it was important for their children to learn to swim because of the many water channels in the area into which they might fall and drown. The parents consulted with the staff of a neighborhood center, who proposed an alternative plan when they learned that no immediate governmental action was forthcoming. Arrangements were made for parents to bus the children to a pool in another part of the city. This attracted wide participation, extensive publicity, and resulted in the organization of similar efforts in other neighborhoods. Members of the City Council heard about the project and were persuaded to give a high priority to the construction of a swimming pool in the area.

ANALYSIS OF SURVEY FINDINGS

> In a small village in South Holland dominated by
> Orthodox Protestant groups, three "unchurched" resi-
> dents became concerned about the lack of a village
> center, playing field, or swimming pool, and com-
> plained that there was nothing for adults or children
> to do. Plays were not permitted, nor was dancing
> sanctioned. They tried to form a committee, but met
> with the objections of the town council, who declared
> that there was no need to provide for such frivolous
> activities. Undaunted, the three organized a meeting
> for the whole population which was opposed by the
> church leaders. The community worker attached to a
> regional council became an advisor to the group and
> investigated the possibility of a regional village
> center. He was able to persuade the municipal execu-
> tive to approve the proposal and apply for a subsidy
> for a regional center: "They now see it's more
> 'pagan' to let people drown in the river than to
> construct a swimming pool."

The major activity and primary function of community
work--regardless of its setting--seems to be the creation of an
infrastructure for community problem-solving. The staff tries
to organize small groups of residents, most often those associated with or representing various religious and cultural interests,
to identify and study problems, and to develop a plan of action,
usually in relation to some physical change or facility. The
scope of issues considered tends to be broader in the rural areas,
where the concept of community is more comprehensive, more geographic, and less specialized, and involves a closer relationship
between economic, social, and political problems. In the rural
areas, there is much greater emphasis on the establishment of a
community center, which is often seen as the primary step in
strengthening the bonds of community identification: "When you
organize associations, people will not support them, but if you
build modern meeting rooms and make playgrounds available, people
will make their own associations." Unfortunately, this strong
belief in community centers as an intrinsically valuable social
utility is not always borne out, because many of the centers are
inadequately staffed and a growth in community identification and
competence does not occur.

The community groups in both rural and urban areas are
more often ad hoc than continuing, and are seen by some community
workers as part of an effort to "democratize Dutch society," although most of the respondents are not very sanguine regarding
these prospects.

Virtually all of the projects, in both old or new neighborhoods or in the cities and towns, are concerned with leisure
time recreation and benefits accruing mainly to children and

youth, although there are several projects involving clubs for
older persons. A few isolated examples are found in the more
rural areas in which the projects are concerned with schools,
the promotion of tourism, or, in one instance, economic development. Most of the projects, however, are exceedingly small in
scope, and some are quite marginal. For example, one worker
described a year-long effort in one of the largest cities in
Holland to persuade the management of a housing project to provide a street-level water tap so that the residents could wash
their cars!

     Some attention is given by the community workers to cer-
tain strained social relationships which are viewed as problematic, such as those between newcomers and oldtimers, "anti-social"
families and more conventional ones, and working-class and middle-
class persons living in a neighborhood. The principal means of
dealing with these relationships is to achieve some diversity
among the members of the committees. This objective is rarely attained, because the participants in most of the community improvement ventures are usually a small hand-picked group of professionals and other high status individuals. (Several neighborhood
groups are quite heterogeneous in their composition, however.)

     The methods and strategies employed are, without excep-
tion, consensual, relying on fact-finding--usually by means of
self-surveys, exchange of information, education, and discussion,
with personal, professional, or political influence occasionally
utilized. Typically, after an extensive process of citizen de-
liberation, letters are sent to a government body, to which
there will be no response. Eventually, the Burgemeester or some
other governmental official will relent, and the requested facility or improvement will be approved. The process can be described
as one of "consumer consultation," which is apparently an inno-
vative and emerging trend in Holland, with the community worker
serving as a social broker between a governmental policy that
provides subsidies and a clientele in need of amenities.

     Over half of the projects eventually achieved their objec-
tives--perhaps because of their relatively simple, noncontroversial nature. Many of them probably would have succeeded without
the intervention of the community worker, although he may have
accelerated the process. For example, many of the projects required "citizen initiative" before a governmental subsidy could
be granted to establish a facility which had already been defined
as in the public interest. Since 1965, governmental subsidies
have been available for community centers when they will serve
the interests of more than one group and are under the sponsorship of a community-wide body with representation from the various
zuilen. In this way, government provides both the funds for the
project goals of the community worker and the technical assistance
to inform and stimulate groups to take advantage of these benefits.

As a result, much community work is concerned with establishing
recreational facilities for children and youth, kindergartens,
day nurseries, and youth centers and associations, and the provision of assembly halls and recreational areas such as playgrounds, green space, and sports fields. Community work is
almost never involved in the provision of housing to meet family
needs, the building of schools, or the provision of churches,
cultural institutions, shopping centers, transportation and
other public services, or hospitals. Community work seems to
be more successful in achieving its objectives in the smaller
communities than in the larger ones, where the political and
social structure is much more complex and there is greater distance between the citizens and the decision-making centers in
the community.

The character and content of the issues and projects with
which community work in Holland is concerned, with their emphasis
on leisure-time needs, should be viewed in the light of these
factors:

(1) Despite extensive planning experience in Holland,
there is still a lack of adequate <u>social</u> planning with respect
to the development of new housing, new neighborhoods, and the
new "mix" of people. This is manifested in the failure to require the corporate sponsors of new, governmentally subsidized
housing to provide those social utilities and amenities long
recognized as essential.

(2) While there is recognition that the lack of community
life may be due to the absence of appropriate facilities, there
are historical reasons imbedded in the religio-political matrix
of Dutch society that militate against the direct provision
of a "public" recreational program. Such facilities can come
into being only as a result of group initiative. Subsidy policy and practices are still influenced by the nineteenth-century
emancipation movements, whereby cultural and recreational programs served as a vehicle for the achievement of identity and
mobility for the various <u>zuilen</u>--including the religious,
trade union, and socialist movements. These groups wanted
and still desire to preserve their identity by keeping out
external influences and maintaining control over their membership, and have traditionally utilized their separate socio-
cultural programs for this purpose. Accordingly, there is
strong opposition to such programs being operated directly by
the government, which would usurp the prerogatives traditionally
held by the religious and socio-economic blocs. Because of
this lack of sanction for direct governmental action, relatively
simple, basic cultural and recreational neighborhood amenities
have to come into being through group action nurtured by community development in each locality rather than through direct
public provision.

(3) Another possible reason for the rather limited scope of community development is that leisure-time needs and somewhat marginal social amenities may be the only unmet needs in an advanced welfare state such as Holland, where it is assumed that the basic economic needs, along with education, housing, and medical care, have been provided for.

(4) A final element that may reinforce the others is the professional background of many of the community workers in social and non-directive group work, which may predispose them to identify and work with those leisure-time problems and needs most familiar to them.

In addition to these factors influencing the character and content of the issues with which community development is concerned, there are internal and external variables affecting it which are the source of many constraints. These include some administrative-organizational factors relating to sponsorship, and some of the socio-political components of the Dutch civic culture and their implications for citizen participation.

Sponsorship

All of the six types of organizational sponsors for community work are subsidized by government, but there is considerable diversity among these quasi-public organizations. The provincial development councils, for example, vary greatly according to name, function, composition, relationship to government, and the scope of their planning. Although some provincial development councils have a history going back to 1926, as in Drenthe, many of the other structures are new, and are a response to legislation passed in 1965. The community workers were about equally divided in their estimation of the provincial development council as a sponsor of community work. Because it contains representatives from the major religious, governmental, and civic groupings, such a high status board is regarded by approximately half of the respondents as a handicap in organizing population groups, and a deterrent to any action that might adversely affect the inter-relationships of the institutional representatives. On the other hand, sponsorship by the provincial development council is regarded by other staff members as a positive factor, particularly when they are assigned to regional councils--mainly because it seems to give them a neutral status in working with the competing and highly parochial villages.

As occasional sponsors of community work, the neighborhood center boards have somewhat more autonomy and are less closely tied to the religio-political structure than the various provincial, regional, and urban development councils, even though many of the former are under the auspices of religious denominations.

What is characteristic of all types of sponsors--provincial, regional, or urban development councils <u>and</u> neighborhood centers--
is that community development is not their primary function. The
neighborhood centers are engaged mainly in direct services, and
the councils have a broad mandate for planning and coordinating
functions among governmental and voluntary agencies with community development--at best, an adjunct to their inter-organizational work.

The relationship between the community worker and his sponsor was specially highlighted in the responses from the neighborhood centers. It is noteworthy how consistently the staff members
expressed the belief that their board members did not know about
or support community work. There is considerable evidence of a
substantial difference in the priority assigned to and the conception of community work between the neighborhood center board and
staff members, as illustrated by the following excerpts from the
interviews:

> I don't think they have any idea about community devel-
> opment. At most, they know it is different than neigh-
> borhood work, but that's all.

> My work is not hampered by the board because they are
> not involved.

> The board is often incompetent, from a professional
> point of view. They think they're experts who know
> what to do, but in general, they don't know what
> they're talking about and have come into their posi-
> tions for all kinds of odd motives.

The disparagement of board members, their motivations, com-
mitments, and capabilities was particularly pronounced among the
staff members of neighborhood centers, who observed that their
board members were mainly concerned with attendance at building-
center recreational programs and short-term visible projects:

> The board is mainly interested in a "full house,"
> and they complain about the smaller clubs.

> When the various councils bring their proposals to
> the board they only ask how much it costs, and if
> it is too expensive, they object.

Many of the community workers chafed at some of the constraints
imposed upon them, and in order to maximize their autonomy, they
devised various stratagems to keep their board members at a distance. Sometimes this would take the form of not informing the
board what they were doing, or disguising it so that it would
appear to be acceptable:

I have the good fortune that a lot of my duties and
work are not clear to the board, so they don't pay
much attention. For example, accounts and reports
are never read by most of the board members.

As a professional, you ought to be free to do as you
want.

Several workers told about colleagues who had tried to organize
neighborhood groups, but who had been pressured by their sponsors
to desist. It was claimed that several workers had resigned for
this reason.

The linkages of the sponsoring organization to government
provide both advantages and disadvantages for the community workers. On the one hand, the linkage with the government provides
access to useful information and a structural means for communication between citizens and their government. On the other hand,
community work's connection with government may lead to suspicion
and skepticism on the part of the citizenry. It may reinforce
their traditional indifference, since they may assume that the
community worker has great influence with the government, and
hence there is no need for the involvement of ordinary people:
"They're used to letting others do the work. If someone wants
to do something for you, you'd be crazy not to let them."

Some of the sponsoring agencies claim to be in a position
to make recommendations to local government regarding social welfare and other types of subsidies. This could be a source of
leverage on various agencies. It was often reported, however,
that local government is usually not interested in the recommendations of community workers and their agencies regarding subsidies. Even in communities with well-established councils, such
as those in the larger cities, it was asserted that local government did not refer important issues to the council and bypassed
them in the political struggle over subsidies. From a practice
perspective, however, implementation of the government's subsidy
policies seems to be one of the most significant determinants of
the character of community work. Subsidy policy is the source
of many of the inter-organizational and community development
goals, as well as the source of many of the problems which it is
expected to ameliorate. One of the major goals of the provincial
development councils, for example, is rooted in the expectation
that community organization can bring together the atomistic,
uncoordinated network of social welfare services whose fragmented
pattern is supported by the subsidy policy. In this way, the
subsidy serves as one of the chief incentives for inter-organiza-
tion collaboration: "We tackle the problems [cooperation among
agencies] by referring to the conditions. Cooperation; otherwise
you can't get a subsidy." One regional council staff member described the community image of his sponsoring organization as

"a place where you can get the money." In addition to the sponsor functioning as a funnel for those subsidies which determine the specific content of the goals of community work, such as recreational facilities and other amenities which citizens are enabled to obtain, the sponsoring organization is itself subsidized. Perhaps this explains why so few of the community workers reported any instances of conflict in their practice. Dependency on the subsidy and the goodwill of government seems to require a strategy of conflict-avoidance, i.e., avoidance of controversial and hence important issues which might result in political opposition.

In addition to the influence upon community work of these relationships to its sponsor and to subsidy policies, the _locus_ of community work has a significant effect on its character, role, and influence. Locality serves as the primary power base around which citizens are organized, and from which they operate. Because community development seeks to organize citizens on the basis of their residence, it is more dependent on the strength of a person's attachment to place than his religious or political affiliation or social status. However, local associations seem to have little appeal and continuity, partly because there is a high degree of mobility in most of the neighborhoods. As a result, the viability of territoriality as the basis of organization in Holland has increasingly been called into question.[1]

Locality, or the horizontal orientation of community work, means that it is outside the primary, vertical structures of religio-political power, which are highly centralized--both in the various _zuilen_ and in the government. The absence of a linkage to these influential structures may explain both the choice of issues and the low potential of community work as a force for change.

This brings us to the other internal factor (apart from the sponsoring organization) which influences community work-- namely, the professionals themselves. The professional community workers include two types of persons, with about an equal division between them: (1) former social workers, who are graduates of schools of social work (or "Social Academies," as they are called) which are not connected with the universities, and (2) university-

---

[1]A thoughtful statement of the limitations of locality as the basis of community organization in the more developed countries is Sj. Groenman, "Social Development on a Territorial Basis"-- excerpts from a booklet published by The Netherlands Association for Social and Cultural Educational Work, n.d. Also see his article "Community Development in Urban Areas," _International Review of Community Development_, Vol. 7 (1961), pp. 61-69.

educated sociologists and a few political science graduates. The former have had a background of either casework or nondirective group work, which may explain their emphasis on process and leisure-time goals, and the absence of specified long-range objectives. There are significant status and value differentials between the two types of community workers reflecting their social origins and educational backgrounds. Many of the community workers who are former social workers are strongly influenced by certain American values and traditions implicit in their training. They contrast with their university-educated colleagues, who tend to be more assertive, politically sophisticated, and somewhat less concerned with interpersonal relationship processes. The governmental administrators and planners with whom the community workers deal occasionally are similar to the university graduates, and do not share the social workers' beliefs in the values of citizen participation or in the role of nondirective agents of change.

While both types of community workers see their roles as primarily "enablers" and technical assistants to citizen groups, they seldom regard it as their function to point out a wider range of alternatives than those promoted by their governmental sponsor. Typical of many comments are these:

> I informed them what way should be chosen. . .;
> actually, I am too active. For example, if they
> want to talk with the city council, I must go with
> them. I also have to take the minutes, give speeches,
> and make reports because they aren't able to do these
> things. It's a pity.

> The council (alas!) has to think for the region
> since it is not able to do this by itself.

There were few indications of any consideration of opposition to public policy as a possibility. Instead, the community workers generally seek to facilitate adjustment to or compliance with a set of conditions or goals formulated by the national government. They inform the population what is being planned and how they can accommodate themselves to the changes. Their efforts appear to be directed more toward administrative involvement and the engineering of consent rather than the more open process of problem identification and examination of alternatives. As a result, much community development is concerned with changing the behavior of individuals who comprise a client system deemed in need of modification because of public policy. Since virtually all planning is centralized in Holland, community development frequently becomes a means to influence the population to cooperate and fit in with planned programs considered to be in the national interest, such as industrialization, the conversion of agricultural land to residential or industrial use, airport expansion, etc.

As agents of and brokers for government, it is notable
that the community workers, like their Israeli counterparts, manifest relatively little of the role strain that might be expected
between professionals and the bureaucracies that employ them.[2]
This could be explained in terms of the congruence between their
goals and those of their sponsor, both of whom share the same
culture and commitment to national policy. Another interpretation
of the lack of conflict which is often found between professionals
and their sponsoring, bureaucratic organizations is that the professionalism of the community worker is of a low order. Many of
them are new to their jobs, do not have a common professional
background, and do not enjoy high status or power in the social
hierarchy in most communities.

Civic Culture

The second set of factors influencing the character and
outcomes of community work pertains to several elements of the
civic culture including (1) the role of _verzuiling_, (2) the political system, and (3) the socio-cultural norms for citizen
participation.

(1) It can now be seen that the religio-political institutions serve as the dominant context, sponsor, and target for community work. Community workers face the typical practice dilemma
whereby the same institutions on which they depend for legitimation, support, access, and resources for influence are also the
chief sources of resistance to their professional and organizational goals. This is particularly true in the case of the pillarized structures for social welfare, which contribute to the
problematic conditions of "over-organization and over-institution-
alization" to which much of community work is addressed. In those
communities where _verzuiling_ is strongly entrenched, the possibilities for the creation of new, de-pillarized voluntary associations
are quite limited. Under these circumstances, community workers
have little choice except to work within the system, recognizing
the centrality of religious attachments as they try to convene
representatives of the various _zuilen_ in an effort to educate
and change them in the desired direction. In this way, bypassing
the unchurched and concentrating almost exclusively on the existing religious structure and trying to modify it, it is believed
by some that community work can help strengthen the forces of
emancipation within at least two of the three major religious
groups. This is sometimes elevated into a rationale for community work, i.e., that one should start with the existing structure,
taking people and their communities "where they are," and involve

---

[2]See references in footnote 11, p. 35 **above**.

citizens coming from closed patterns into a structure which is
not determined by traditional but by evolving values. The efficacy of this strategy, however, remains to be assessed, and it
may well be the case that, as one respondent said:

> After all these fine talks, people fall back on their
> own small world, not willing to solve the intergroup
> problems of cooperation with other religious and non-
> religious groups.

As a result, it is difficult to see how opportunities for inter-
denominational collaboration can weaken the process which is used
as the basis of representation, i.e., _verzuiling_. Rather, it appears that community work, particularly its inter-organizational
aspect, would reinforce the existing pattern rather than contribute to de-pillarization. The latter goal may be another example
of the overreach of community work in setting up objectives
beyond its capabilities.

Regardless of the extent of _verzuiling_ in a local community, the various _zuilen_ have formidable influence on the provincial and national levels, where most of the important decisions
are made affecting the various social services under their auspices. As the primary resource system for the provision of most
social services, the _zuilen_ cannot be overlooked or bypassed.
Since it is very difficult to create an "unchurched" group which
can secure adequate private financing, community workers are quite
dependent on the various religious groups for the funding of any
new needed service. Or the cooperation of the _zuilen_ as representative of various community interests may be required in order
to qualify for government financing, particularly for various
facilities and amenities. In these ways, then, _verzuiling_ continues to shape the practice of community work.

(2) The concept of the civic culture has as its core the
attitudes and behaviors pertaining to the world of politics among
various groups in the society. The survey data suggest how the
political system is perceived by the community workers. Their
dominant attitudes are that the political system is a major source
of strain because it is so sluggish, unresponsive, and disinterested in community work and citizen participation:

> The political system and the local governmental agen-
> cies aren't accustomed to or ready for the democratic
> influence of the people.

> The political parties don't help or hinder community
> work because they just don't pay much attention to it.

> Most of the questions are put before the municipal
> councils by me, but nothing is done.

Local government doesn't like "trouble" from the residents. They like the residents to organize leisure
time activities and festivals, but not to take any
action regarding their living situation.

Political or controversial issues are avoided by virtually
all of the groups staffed by community workers, and pressure on
government is usually limited to the use of formal channels such
as sending letters, although informal contacts are occasionally
initiated with officials. Contacts with the political system
seem to be more frequent and intensive in the rural areas, with
municipal governments quite remote in the cities and towns. Many
of the community workers have informal relationships with politicians, and it has become increasingly acceptable to make such
contacts. Several of the community workers expressed a view of
their function as that of adult educators helping citizens to
better understand the operation of their government. A minority
of the respondents believe that community work is essentially
political. More common is the view that community workers have
little to do with politics and that they should be avoided--a
conception that is reinforced by the professional ideology of
community development and the training of the staff:

Why should one talk about politics? We never do in
the working groups.

I am glad that the people aren't willing to talk about
politics, because these matters are really obscure to
them.

There are no connections between the members of the
discussion groups and the city council members.

Most of the respondents view government as a source of funds and
legitimation for their goals, even though local government is
regarded by them as having a very low commitment to democratic
values. Most government officials are described by the community
workers as intensely parochial, narrow in their views, and authoritarian (or at best, paternalistic) in action. The respondents
make repeated references to the bureaucratic tradition of not
consulting with the people directly or even informing them of
decisions which affect them:

Good information from the local authorities is necessary. But the question is "Who is going to give them
this information?" Civil servants are not policy
makers, and they always have to consult their Alder-
man. That is why the population does not know how
the government works. That is also why civil servants
have a tendency to keep things secret even in cases
when it is not necessary. . . . I think that it should

> be possible to have public discussion about different
> matters, and that the civil servant should have the
> right to intervene and advise Aldermen so that the
> population can see how the system works and to whom
> they should address their wishes.[3]

Some community workers believe that their work is viewed as a
threat by politicians, who regard the structures for community
work as unrepresentative, with little accountability and of
limited usefulness:

> The College of Burgemeester and Wethouders believe that
> my work of promoting discussion and cooperation is of
> minor importance. They don't even talk about or read
> my reports. Much more important than a sports center
> or social work to them is the promotion of industriali-
> zation.

In many of the regional development councils and local communities, the Burgemeester is almost invariably a board member, and
he is viewed by most of the community workers as one of the main
obstacles to their work: "The municipal boards don't believe in
fundamental democratization, and the Burgemeester is a patriarch
in most villages and towns." In general, community workers believe that inclusion of political officials on the boards of the
sponsors of community work means that little can be done that
does not meet with their approval. At the same time, they recognize how necessary such officials are in helping them accomplish
their tasks.

There are some important exceptions to the essentially
apolitical character of community work. One is in Rotterdam.
Here, community work was involved for almost six years in a struggle with political parties over the right to organize nonpartisan
welfare planning councils in neighborhoods which had advisory
boards composed of representatives from the various political
parties. The Rotterdam community work staff argued that the
political councils had no competence in the field of social welfare, and that they represented only the small proportion of less
than 10 percent of the voters belonging to the political parties.
The Rotterdam Council of Social Welfare claimed that _its_ pattern
of organization was more democratic:

> The aim of the council is to draw as many private
> citizens as possible into running their own community.

---

[3]Interview with A. de Gier, City Planner of Amsterdam, printed
in _NIMO Bulletin_, No. 2 (April 1968), p. 11 (translated by T.
Hijna).

> By encouraging public participation we succeed in
> developing more democracy. As the public takes an
> active part in democracy, . . . the general discom-
> fort will diminish.[4]

It proposed the formation of district councils comprised of representatives of all interest groups and associations within each
district. Each council would consist of several sections (social
work, education, sports, culture, unions, political parties) to
which each group would send a delegate. A compromise was finally
agreed to whereby the political councils would have a health and
welfare section and the district councils would have a political
section which would advise the city on health and welfare matters,
with the political councils making recommendations on administrative and nonspecialized social welfare issues.

The Rotterdam Department of Social and Community Work
was recently reorganized, and its leadership is highly politicized. The Director of Social Work is a former member of Parliament, and the Director of Community Work is an active member of
the Socialist Party with many contacts in political circles.

(3) Related to the role of the political system are certain socio-cultural attributes of the population about whose
constraining effects on community work there is little disagreement. The community workers spoke again and again about the
"apathy" of their clientele--regardless of their social class,
rural or urban residence, or religious affiliation:

> The population is really not fit to take the initia-
> tive. They want to work only for very short periods
> of time. Emotionally, they can get enthusiastic, but
> maintaining organization on a long-term basis is
> almost impossible, partly because of a rapid depar-
> ture of young families and partly because of person-
> ality factors.

> The people are more or less the same. There are no
> local leaders, which makes it difficult to reach
> them. That's why you can only work with other pro-
> fessionals.

> The people neither see nor think about the problems.
> . . . I have to push them to fill their lives by

---

[4]Data on community organization in Rotterdam were derived from
interviews and the following sources: European Meeting of Community Development Trainers, pp. 59-62, and Maas-Mondig, published
by the Rotterdam Council of Social Welfare, Vol. 1, Nos. 1 and 2
(January and February 1968).

> being involved and not to be fatalistic. They have
> to make their contribution. . . . The intellectual
> level isn't too high, but they're clever enough to
> be able to express themselves.

> Although people are in general dissatisfied about com-
> munity and existing facilities, they have little moti-
> vation to participate in a community process. I think
> this is due to a lack in our educational system and
> the unwillingness of government to deliberate with the
> residents about facilities. People are just not accus-
> tomed to have influence in the community.

> Community development really has no future. I doubt
> if the Ministry or NIMO officials know about resis-
> tance in the rural areas to discussing the future.

There are numerous complaints about the lack of preparation, training, motivation, and capabilities for citizen participation in Holland. These values are not stressed in family life,
schools, or in any of the other institutions, most of which still
have a rather pronounced traditionalist or even authoritarian
character:

> The main problem is the apathy of the people in old
> city areas and their lack of courage to take initia-
> tives. Their daily life, their jobs, and their
> environment are responsible for this passivity. In
> the factory they have always done what the boss says
> because he knows more. In most situations these
> people meet others who are more knowledgeable, skilled,
> and powerful.

Many community workers claim that they are trying to
promote "modern" values in the traditional Dutch society, but
they find relatively little discontent and much powerlessness
in the population--particularly in the poor and working class
neighborhoods, where many of the inhabitants are stigmatized.
In general, people are believed to be unaware of their rights
and the possibilities of action, regarding themselves more as
subjects than as citizens: "Even the middle class people don't
like to be involved. The businessmen are afraid to lose their
customers and aren't willing, for example, to permit posters
for any political parties or events to be hung in their windows."

In many of the rural areas where regional development
councils operate, religious orthodoxy remains prevalent, and
events such as Sunday recreation or dancing may still be regarded
as "the work of the devil." The attitudes in these areas are
very difficult to change, and much effort is expended in trying
to awaken the people to the meaning of the social changes taking

place in their midst. Because of the distance between the people
and their government, and the absence of programs of problem-
centered adult education, the community worker may play an important role in bringing information regarding social trends, public
policy, and some of the possibilities for coping with these
changes.

A Note on Inter-organizational Work

Before describing the future plans for community work,
it might be helpful to note briefly some impressions of its inter-
organizational aspects. Utilizing the structure of a council of
agency delegates, the coordinating bodies convene representatives
of the various denominational sponsors of social welfare services.
These organizations are often considered to be an expression of
citizen participation as articulated in the ideology of community
development, but in fact they involve a very small, self-selected
elite who represent a pillarized, functional community rather
than the geographic community, even though they may speak in the
name of the latter.

Like their counterparts in the United States and elsewhere, these councils seem to lack the appropriate mandate and
authority to induce productive collaboration, and they are constrained by the very conditions that sustain them. The various
community organization councils, for example, do not enjoy a
monopoly on the sanction to seek coordination, but must compete
with similar and usually much older and more powerful organizations under the auspices of the various zuilen. As an illustration, in the Ymond area there are seven different coordinating
agencies for social welfare on the municipal level. In addition,
there are usually separate planning councils for different fields
of service, such as health, recreation, and youth services, sponsored by both the zuilen and the newer subsidized organizations.
The latter seem to have little leverage with local agencies, whose
authority is limited and whose policies are determined nationally
by the various central institutions of which they are a part.

On the assumption that communication difficulties rather
than competing interests block coordination, the development
councils rely on voluntary collaboration among organizational
interest groups--many of whom are either threatened by the councils or are sufficiently autonomous to be able to ignore them.
Nor do these councils seem to have much influence over the primary
sources of financing within the local-national governmental structure. There also appears to be relatively little coordination
between social welfare and other sectors, perhaps because the
pattern of religious representation which pervades social welfare
has little sanction in the organizational structures concerned
with physical and economic planning. The result is a vast and

complex apparatus preoccupied with structural and representational problems which seems to produce relatively little in the way of community planning and change, but which gives the appearance of participation and cooperation.[5]

Future Plans

The present pattern of community work is viewed by some officials of the Ministry of Cultural Affairs, Recreation and Social Welfare (CRM) as an interim one, or as only a first step toward the implementation of an ambitious, long-range, two-pronged effort of community organization and development which would require at least a six-fold increase in the number of professional staff. This long-range plan envisages a hierarchical model of social planning on the neighborhood, district, city, regional, provincial, and national levels, with each feeding in information and recommendations to the next level. On the grass-roots or neighborhood level, there are plans to develop more of a social and cultural infrastructure by greater utilization of the staffs of neighborhood centers working directly with residents, rather than by reliance on the detached staff from urban, regional, or provincial councils. On the municipal and provincial levels, an effort will be made within the next five years to require the establishment of social planning bodies, somewhat similar to community welfare councils in the United States, whose recommendations regarding social welfare services would have to be published and considered by the municipal and/or provincial government. It would be expected that only those programs would be subsidized which had been recommended by the planning councils, although there would be provision for agencies to appeal the actions of local government. Some beginning steps to implement this plan have been taken in Rotterdam, Enschede, and Amsterdam, where six

---

[5]In discussions of inter-agency coordination in Holland, there is relatively little attention given to some of the more recent conceptions of coordination, its costs and prerequisites. Instead, there is an over-reliance on some of the ideas formulated over twenty years ago, when much less was known about the ways in which inter-organizational coordination might constrain citizen participation. Representative of some recent work in this field are the following in Kramer and Specht, eds., Readings in Community Organization Practice: William J. Reid, "Inter-organizational Coordination in Social Welfare: A Theoretical Approach to Analysis and Intervention," pp. 176-188; Saul Levine, Paul E. White, and Benjamin D. Paul, "Community Inter-organizational Problems in Providing Medical Care and Social Services," pp. 162-175; and Martin Rein and Robert Morris, "Goals, Structures, and Strategies for Community Change," pp. 188-200.

experimental projects have been authorized. In general, CRM is
quite optimistic about the prospects for community development.

While the intent to implement a more consistent and comprehensive social policy and to strengthen democracy by stimulating citizen participation in these new community structures is
laudable, the experience with similar efforts in the United States
is not an encouraging one. Any attempt to develop a structure
which would include both geographic and functional representation
and, within the latter, would cut across denomination and fields
of service lines is a most formidable undertaking in Holland.
The history of similar experiences in community welfare planning
and neighborhood organization is, regrettably, not sufficiently
well known in Holland, where there is a tendency to overestimate
the degree of effectiveness of community organization in the
United States. In many ways the cleavages and fragmentation within the social welfare community are greater in Holland than in
the United States, and there is much less sanction and support
for citizen participation in social planning than in America.

Nevertheless, CRM continues to rely on the community
organization and development processes to develop alternative or
at least countervailing de-pillarized councils to bring a greater
measure of rationality and democracy into the social planning
process. CRM officials regard the shortage of professional personnel as the critical threat to their future program, although
the absence of sufficient support by the religio-political power
structure is recognized as an important factor. In relation to
the latter, CRM appears to be somewhat at a disadvantage because
of its position in the middle--between the _zuilen_ and the government, which is itself pillarized. Representing largely a set of
professional-bureaucratic values, goals, and interests, with no
distinct constituency of its own, CRM appears to be in a politically weak bargaining position. CRM is dependent on the _zuilen_
who, because they can define their own markets, producers, and
consumers, have a practical monopoly on the service products which
are subsidized by the government. Understandably, CRM may be reluctant to use its limited standard-setting and financing powers
on the confessional blocs who constitute private governments in
themselves and who have direct links with the national government
through their own political parties.

Under these circumstances, the ability of CRM to promote
its long-range proposals will be a test of the relative strengths
of the competing values and interests of the _zuilen_ and the social
planning bureaucrats and professionals.

Chapter VI

SUMMARY AND CONCLUSIONS

Community work in Holland can refer to three different
modes of practice: (1) inter-organizational work, a form of
social planning which is often considered synonymous with community development; (2) buurtwerk, a form of group work in the
neighborhood; and (3) "authentic" community development, in which
the goal is to organize people in a locality who are directly affected by a problem condition to take some action regarding it.
Although most of the community work resources in Holland are al-
located to inter-organizational work, it is the third type--com-
munity development--which is the primary focus of this exploratory study.

Rooted in the pillarized structure of social work and in
social planning efforts in the underdeveloped parts of the country, community work is completely subsidized by the government
and is sponsored by quasi-public, council-type structures on five
different geographical levels. The provincial, regional, and
urban development councils, as well as the neighborhood centers,
provide staff for community development purposes to small localities. The major goals for the community work enterprise are
based on maximizing the values of social welfare rationality and
modernization by means of citizen participation. The primary
methods for achieving these goals are to create an infrastructure
for problem-solving and to develop projects which will enable
residents to obtain selected amenities.

A survey of 46 community development workers revealed
that the workers' perception of community problems in both urban
and rural settings is usually limited to a narrow range of public
facility lacks, along with concern about the low civic competence
of the population. The urban workers' usual response to a problem is to convene small groups of the more active residents to
conduct a self-survey and/or formally request the establishment
of a leisure-time facility. Because of the requirements of
verzuiling and the subsidy policy, which mitigate against direct
governmental provision of services, the formation of citizen initiative groups is often the only way that many social utilities
can be obtained. In this way, the community workers help implement public policy by serving as social brokers beteen a clientele
in need of amenities, and the subsidy program. In the more rural
areas, where the concept of community and scope of issues is somewhat broader, the dominant emphasis is on the establishment of

facilities such as community centers and/or efforts to stimulate
the villagers to adapt themselves to the rapid social changes
that are occurring in their region.

The issues and projects with which the community development workers are associated are rarely controversial, and consensual methods are relied upon almost exclusively for educating
citizens and informing officials. There is some recognition of
the existence of strained social relationships among various population groups, but the typical community development project seems
to have little impact on the religious and social class stratification that pervades Dutch community life. Most of the community
development groups are ad hoc and project-centered, and though
they usually achieve their task goals, there appears to be relatively little continuity, grass-roots involvement, leadership
development, or the increased collaborative competence expected
in a community development process. For this reason, much of the
community work can better be described as consumer consultation,
social brokerage, or a form of group work transferred to a micro-
community level, rather than as authentic community development
with a potential for democratizing Dutch society, as is sometimes
claimed.

The distinctive character of the goals and methods of
community development strongly reflect (1) its micro-area locus,
(2) its sponsors and their relationship to the government that
subsidizes them, and (3) the religio-political matrix within which
it functions, including the civic culture.

(1) There is a preoccupation with leisure-time needs,
almost to the exclusion of all others, in part as a consequence
of the micro-area locus of practice of community development.
Recreational and cultural facilities are among the few benefits
that can be obtained through locality-based citizen initiative.
Because of the high degree of centralization in a small country,
there are few social problems amenable to local action within the
Dutch institutional structure. Recognition of other needs is
hindered by the existence of a multiplicity of agencies, the relatively low degree of public discontent, and the professional pre-
dispositions of the staff.

(2) The role and influence of community development is
shaped by its organizational sponsors, many of which are new and
external to--yet dependent on--the pillarized structure of social
welfare. The linkage of the development councils to government
provides an important channel for communication between citizens
and their public officials, but at the same time it may lead to
suspicion and skepticism on the part of the clientele of the community worker. There is some evidence that community development
programs do not have strong support or understanding among the
board members of neighborhood centers and in the development

councils. In the latter, the presence of institutional representatives and government officials on the policy-making boards is believed to inhibit controversial forms of practice that might lead to community change. Similarly, dependence on the subsidy policy and the goodwill of government seems to require the strategy of avoiding controversy and political issues--a strategy consistently pursued by virtually all community workers. This apolitical orientation and emphasis on consensus are reinforced by the professional ideology of community development and the training of staff members. There were exceptionally few instances in which the staff gave any encouragement to public opposition to government policy. Nor do they seem to articulate alternatives which are outside the range of those sought by the government. Functioning characteristically as amenity brokers, the staff move more often in the direction of administrative involvement of citizens than of substantive participation. This may explain the relative lack of conflict between their professional goals and those of their bureaucratic sponsors.

(3) The pillarized religio-political institutional structure in Holland is the dominant context, sponsor, and resource for community development, as well as its principal target and leading source of resistance. _Verzuiling_, as the general basis of community structure, leadership and participation, and services, cannot be bypassed except in the newer, more urbanized areas. Even here, there are many difficulties involved in working within or around the _zuilen_, whose values and interests often conflict with those of community development. In addition, the staff are confronted with a political system considered unresponsive and quite disinterested in community work and citizen participation, both of which may be perceived as threatening or irrelevant. The possibilities of creating new channels of communication, of heightening social awareness and involvement in community problem-solving, are circumscribed by the low degree of civic competence widely attributed to the Dutch, one of the products of a culture with few norms for citizen participation outside the _zuilen_. This traditional civic culture is reinforced by widespread attitudes of indifference to political issues and deference to authority. Together with the declining significance of locality, these socio-cultural factors contribute to the difficulties in creating new, autonomous, and continuing voluntary associations which are the principal organizational means of attaining the goals of community development.

Conclusions

On the basis of these findings, what conclusions can be drawn about the prospects for community development in Holland? It should first be stated that if this study has stressed the socio-political and organizational constraints on community development, it is because these structural factors are often neglected, not because of any intent to devalue community work practice. It may be that if greater attention is directed to the strength of the forces shaping the character, role, and influence of community work, a more realistic set of expectations can be derived. This study suggests that more limited outcomes should be anticipated from the investments in community development in light of the nature of its socio-political context, organizational sponsors, professional functionaries, and their clientele.

With respect to the inter-organizational aspects of community work, there is some impressionistic evidence that their prospects may also be more constricted than is usually acknowledged. There seems to be insufficient leverage to produce the desired degree of coordination, coherence, and control over the fragmented and pillarized pattern of the social services. The complex, decentralized, federated structures for planning and coordination on the various geographic levels need more powerful sanctions and resources for influence before they can develop a countervailing or even a supplementary system for social planning. The likelihood for acquiring a more effective mandate is related to the prospects for increased de-pillarization in Holland and modification of the subsidy policies which would permit more governmental control over the direct administration of the social services. Unless this occurs in a substantial form, the degree of rationality and effectiveness of the service delivery system can probably not be increased significantly. Even then, experience with the use of voluntary federations of competing interest groups for planning purposes leads one to be less than sanguine regarding the possibilities of coordination.

The prognosis for community development practice is also not very favorable, although this may be less true in the rural areas. It is difficult to see how, under the present circumstances, community development can be more than a form of social brokerage, involving a very small number of citizens in rather peripheral neighborhood-improvement activities. Located outside the prevailing community decision-making structures and yet dependent on them, community development does not appear to have a strong enough power base to approximate its goals, assuming that they are not hortatory but are meant to be taken seriously. As presently conceived, structured, and provisioned, community development can only fulfill its promise on exceedingly minor issues, and cannot be much of a force for change in democratizing Dutch society or modifying social relationships and institutional policies and practice. At best, it can be another mild secularizing and modernizing influence, a minor form of community education in a highly stratified, institutionalized, and centralized social system. To be capable of even a modest impact on community structure and function, the community development program would require relatively unambiguous and feasible objectives, a

cadre of adequately trained, committed, and skilled personnel
with a more versatile professional ideology, and organizational
sponsors with a greater degree of autonomy than is currently possible. Even then it is not clear how community development could
generate sufficient incentives for effective citizen participation,
help nurture a more receptive civic culture, and obtain the resources for influence that would be necessary.

All this suggests that group work and administrative
involvement are quite feasible in Holland, but that it may be
difficult to achieve the broader goals and forms of citizen participation envisioned in community development.

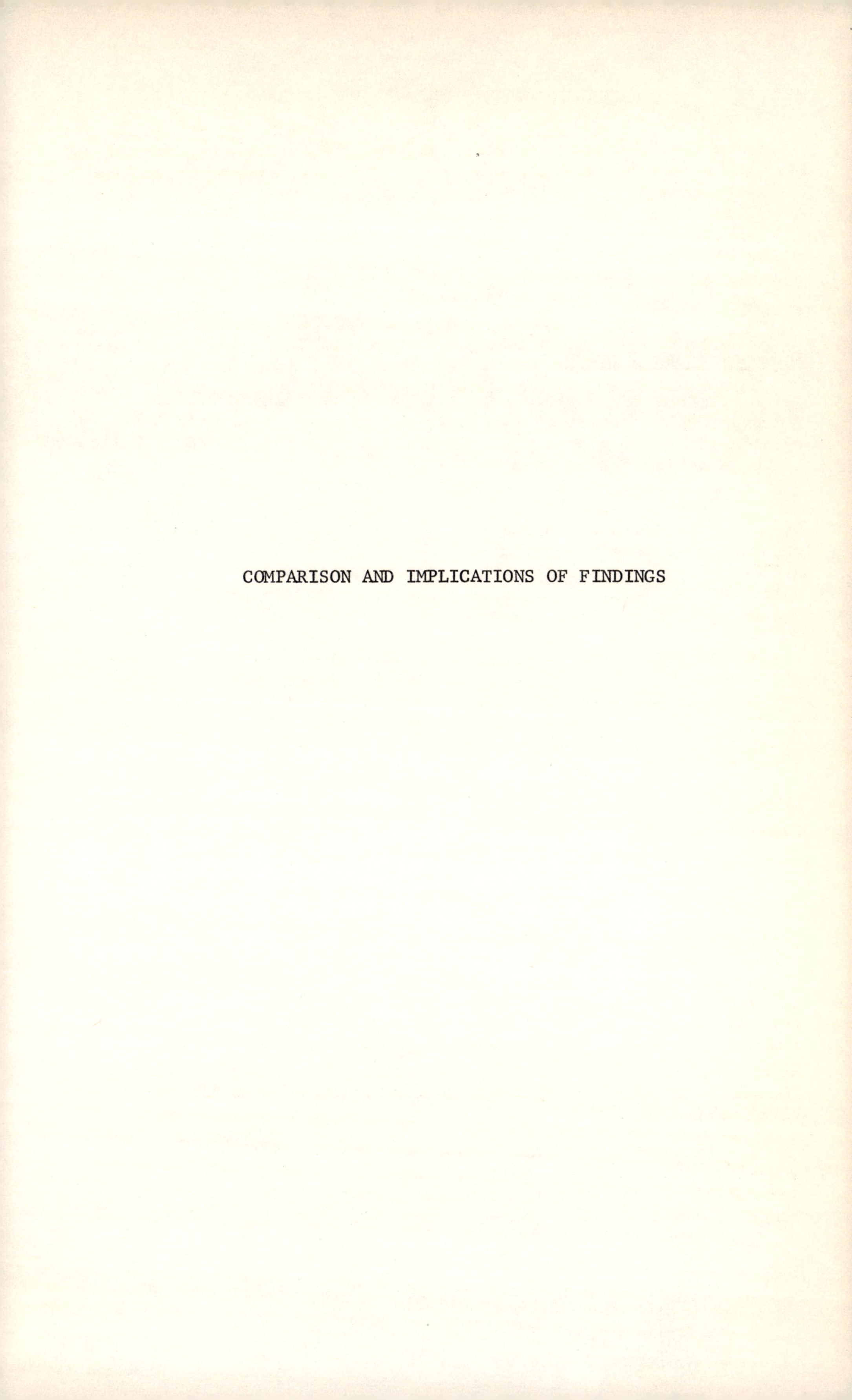

COMPARISON AND IMPLICATIONS OF FINDINGS

Chapter VII

COMPARATIVE ANALYSIS OF COMMUNITY WORK IN ISRAEL
AND THE NETHERLANDS

Sociopolitical Context

Israel and Holland are very small, urbanized, welfare democracies characterized by pervasive, historical social cleavages based on religion and, in Israel, on cultural grounds. While there is a high degree of stratification, both societies are stable and relatively well-integrated despite their segmented character. In both countries there is a complex network of organizations and agencies sponsored by their national institutional structures for their adherents. In Holland these institutional structures are the zuilen. Their counterparts in Israel are the political parties, all of which are highly centralized and concerned with virtually all aspects of their members' lives.

Israel is one of the most politicized of all democracies, with the predominance of power vested in a few highly centralized bureaucratic and political institutions. The national government is also the dominant force in Holland, but there is a much stronger tradition of local autonomy, private ownership, and individualism than in Israel, where the state is the largest landowner, employer, and direct provider of social services. The government of Israel penetrates all phases of its citizens' lives. In Holland the national government is the principal funding source for social services, but not the preferred provider.

Because both countries are so small, most social problems in Holland and Israel are defined nationally, with very few issues considered appropriate for local community action. As a result, there is relatively little power residing in the localities, where community work is practiced; instead, decision-making is concentrated within a political system which, because of its pattern of party lists and proportional representation, is quite removed from direct popular control. Perhaps most significant, there is little or no sanction for independent pressure or interest groups to function outside the established structures for public decision-making.

In both Holland and Israel, the environment is largely man-made, with extensive national planning--particularly in the control of natural resources, agriculture, and, in Israel, the general economy. While Holland is an old, established state with a predominantly native, homogeneous population[1] and an advanced industrial economy, Israel is only 22 years old, has been under continuous attack since its establishment, is comprised of immigrants from 80 countries, and has a developing economy. In both countries most of the leading structural and cultural features of modernization and secularization have emerged in varying degrees, but traditionalism persists and underlies many value conflicts between the old and the new. Both have developed new towns and have had to face many problems because of the population movement <u>into</u> them (in Holland) and <u>out</u> of them (in Israel), with community work utilized as one of the responses to the problems. Accommodation between the religious denominations in Holland has evolved slowly and peacefully over a 300-year period. Israel, a consciously created state, emerged out of unprecedented conditions of genocide during World War II, and its diverse cultural groups from Afro-Asian and European countries have been unified rapidly through the "in-gathering of exiles" and Arab attacks.

Despite marked differences in their origin and composition, there is considerable similarity between the civic cultures of Holland and Israel, and those aspects of the social structure and political environment that are of special significance for community work. In both countries, a lack of suitable norms for citizen participation outside the established political party structure is combined with a strong traditionalist attitude toward authority, which is rooted in religious orthodoxy among Afro-Asian immigrants in Israel and Catholics and neo-Calvinist Protestants in Holland. The patterns of socialization in family, church, and school tend to be authoritarian, providing little preparation and support for democratic participation, which results in rather low civic efficacy.

There is a much higher degree of community structure in Holland than in Israel: over half of the adults belong to various associations sponsored by the <u>zuilen</u>. In Israel, although a large proportion of the population belong to unions, there is a dearth of voluntary agencies and associations of the kind long known in Holland. Much more dissatisfaction with living conditions and greater impatience with government is expressed in Israel than in Holland, but in neither country is the political structure regarded as oppressive, illegitimate, or totally unresponsive. Holland is an affluent country, predominantly middle class, while in Israel one-fourth of the post-establishment immigrants are still "unabsorbed" and require financial aid or welfare services. There is a wide gap in income, housing, and education between the

---

[1]The population is approximately four times as large as that of Israel.

early European immigrants to Israel and more recent ones from
Afro-Asian countries. The strain between these two groups is
intensified by sociocultural differences which involve language
and customs. (Like religious stratification in Holland, these
differences are steadily diminishing.) Both societies are becoming more secular and modern, as is particularly evident in
the larger urban centers and among the younger generation. Nevertheless, stratification persists on the basis of religion and
class in Holland, and in Israel on ethnicity as well, and is one
of the most distinguishing characteristics of these societies.

Sponsors of Community Work

Although rooted in different types of formal organizational structures, the sponsors of urban community work in both countries rely exclusively on government financing. In Holland, six
types of quasi-public welfare planning councils and a form of
neighborhood group work are subsidized by one ministry (CRM),
while in Israel community work is a small department in two large
government bureaucracies--Social Welfare and Housing. In both
countries, the sponsors determine the goals of community work and
the policies to be implemented. Community work is largely a form
of agency-community relations and program development in Israel.
In Holland, implementation of the subsidy policy of the government
serves as an important incentive for participation. In both
countries community work has been sanctioned for approximately
fifteen years, but it is an ancillary and not a primary function
of its sponsors, and relatively limited staff resources are al-
located to it.

The status of community workers is quite low in the local
communities in which they are assigned. They have a higher professional status in the sponsoring ministry in Holland than in
Israel, where the two sponsors are partisan, political in character, and have something of a stigma attached to them. In Holland, most of the community workers are employees of a private
but government-subsidized council, and ultimately accountable to
a board of directors composed of citizens and public officials.
In Israel the community workers are civil servants who are accountable to governmental agency administrators and professional
supervisors.

In both countries community work does not seem to enjoy
much understanding and support within the sponsor's policy-making
structure. Community workers are given a broad mandate by their
sponsors, but they operate largely as agents of the national government in small localities outside the dominant public decision-
making structure and parallel to or superimposed on the local
religious and political structures. They experience little role
strain, perhaps because of the high congruence between their

professional ideology, national goals, and the values and interest of their sponsors, as well as the tenuousness of their professional status.

Goals of Community Work

Despite the differences in organizational structure and historical background, there is a remarkable similarity in the determinants of community work in Holland and Israel. The goals are shaped largely by the governmental sponsor/subsidizer and are implemented through a professional staff which espouses the ideology of community development. In both countries, the task goals focus on the establishment of small-scale social utilities and amenities, with a greater emphasis on leisure-time facilities in Holland than in Israel. The development of infrastructure for micro-community problem-solving is often regarded as an end-in-itself, particularly in Holland. (In Israel the creation of a House Committee in the <u>shikunim</u> is regarded as both a final and an instrumental goal.)

Community work in both countries is characterized by a somewhat hortatory or at least latent concern with "democratizing" the society, and workers in both seek in their distinctive ways to maximize the values of modernization and secularization by overcoming various forms of religious and cultural traditionalism. These broader concerns are a response to rapid social change brought on by the forces of industrialization and urbanization in Holland, and mass immigration and bureaucratic centralization in Israel. In both countries community work is expected to cope in some way with urban migration, and is conceived both as a means of preventing (or at least slowing) the exodus from rural areas and as a method of treating some of the consequences of this exodus.

In Holland, there is a much greater emphasis on social welfare inter-organizational rationality than in Israel, and the role of community work is often thought to be that of coordinating a fragmented social service system. In Israel, acculturation goals are much more significant, and community work is regarded as an integrating instrument of "Israelization," which is primarily a process for absorbing Afro-Asian immigrants into a predominantly European society and polity. While individual and social change objectives are professed by community work, the latter are almost never achieved and the former only occasionally. System maintenance and social control are regarded as more important goals.

Professional Staff

In both countries a small number of community work staff members (less than 50), mainly with backgrounds in various helping professions, but with relatively little specialized professional education for their tasks, are assigned as community workers. They are mostly new to their jobs, many of which have been only recently established. The majority are men in their thirties (in Israel over 40 percent are women) of middle class origin.

There are more college educated workers in Holland, where there is more experience with and opportunity for professional education for community work. In Israel, there is a greater diversity in the professional backgrounds of the staff, and they are subject to much closer supervision than their Dutch counterparts. Even though the workers have a broad mandate and a relatively high degree of autonomy, their professional status in Israel is relatively low and somewhat precarious--in part because their domain is not always recognized by other bureaucracies. Their status is also affected by the lack of a common educational and professional background, as well as the relative newness of the community work program.

In Holland, the professionals are almost equally divided between rural and urban settings, while in Israel community workers are assigned mainly to the neighborhoods in the cities and development towns. Community workers in Israel often face competition for their constituency and in Holland the sponsors also do not have the monopoly on their inter-organizational work.

Both groups of workers espouse the professional ideology of community development, with its emphasis on local self-help, participatory democracy, and community integration by means of consensual and apolitical processes. These professional values tend to conflict with the essential character of the dominant decision-making structures: <u>verzuiling</u> in Holland, and partisan politics in Israel. This strain gives much of the community work in the two countries a distinctive character.

Characteristics of Community Work Practice

The perception by the professionals of the community conditions which are problematic and the selection of issues around which people are organized are influenced mainly by the values and interests of the sponsor and the professional staff rather than by the "felt needs" of the community. Among the most powerful determinants of the issues selected are the implementation of government subsidy policies regarding community centers (in Holland), and concern for property maintenance or public welfare program development (in Israel).

The issues with which community work is concerned are narrow in scope, somewhat marginal and noncontroversial; they usually involve minor neighborhood amenities and improvements.

The focus in Israel is often restricted to basic social utilities related to housing maintenance, although there are a few instances of political and social action. The target system in these efforts is usually the government itself, or the centralized social service bureaucracies. The narrow scope and content of the issues is due in part to the fact that the more salient issues are defined nationally. In Holland the requirements of <u>verzuiling</u> and the subsidy policy, which mitigates against direct governmental provision of service, serve to stimulate the formation of <u>local</u> initiative groups.

In both countries, small numbers of persons are selected by the staff and involved in ad hoc, project-centered groups which use primarily educational and consensual methods to obtain minor amenities from local government (in Holland) and the centralized politicized bureaucracies (in Israel). In part, because these are usually episodic processes and arouse little opposition, they seldom lead to the development of indigenous leadership or organizational continuity.

In both countries, the establishment of a community center is the most frequently reported example of a recent project. Usually because of inadequate financing and staffing, and consequent diminished citizen interest, the achievement of this goal rarely leads to the desired growth in community identification and competence.

The citizen groups are highly dependent on staff assistance to organize and sustain them, and have weak ties both to the broader constituency from which they are drawn as well as to the vertical structures in their respective communities. Their organizational careers are usually short-lived after they obtain the sought-after facility or service improvement, and there is seldom an increase in collaborative capacity. Because of this, <u>much of community work seems to be a form of consumer consultation, social brokerage, or group work on the neighborhood or micro-community level, rather than authentic community development</u>.

As functional bureaucrats in Israel or amenity brokers in Holland, the workers do not seem to articulate alternatives outside the range defined by their governmental sponsors. In Israel, the staff seem to act in a more assertive, unilateral manner as they deliberately pursue predetermined goals, selecting appropriate committee members and suitable issues. They also seem to be more self-critical than their Dutch counterparts, and some are more political, in that they are willing to use pressure tactics in their strategies.

Because of the absence of a tradition of voluntarism and democratic participation, the socializing function of community work in Israel is important. It is a means of helping some of the new citizens become more aware of their rights and opportunities as they learn how to request needed services. Similarly, in Holland, the establishment of social amenities and the educational and informational activities of the community worker have a significant socializing function, particularly in rural areas, within the context of a political system that is quite removed from most citizens.

Constraints and Obstacles

The two major constraints in community work reported by the staff in both countries were essentially similar and pertained to (1) the sociocultural attributes of their client system and (2) the organizational character of the government and/or the dominant public and private bureaucracies.

(1) In both countries the population is deeply divided by religious differences (and in Israel by cultural cleavages) which make it difficult to organize and sustain "mixed" groups. The vested interests of the different _zuilen_ are a powerful inhibiting factor in inter-organizational work in Holland, and the extensive network of voluntary associations supported by the _zuilen_ makes it difficult to organize new associations based on residence. In Israel, there is a cultural stratification reflected in disparities in housing, income, education, and status which the usual community work structures and processes are unable to bridge or affect substantially.

Equally important as an obstacle is the civic culture in each country, which lacks norms for grass-roots participation outside the existing religio-political structure, and where traditionalist, dependent, and deferential attitudes toward authority prevail. The community worker must deal with a population characterized by political disinterest, apathy, and a low order of local community identification.

(2) In both countries, the community workers are confronted by a massive, centralized set of institutions which serves as their context, sponsor, and resource, as well as the leading source of resistance. Unresponsive local governments and/or the rigidities and inefficiencies of "bureaupathic" public or private agencies comprise the principal organizational obstacle to the achievement of community work goals in Holland and Israel. In Holland, the multiplicity of agencies under diverse religious auspices is a special difficulty, while in Israel the highly partisan political character of the community environment and the public bureaucracy constitutes the most serious hindrance. For some Israeli community workers, the stigma and restrictiveness of their sponsor are also formidable constraints.

Other constraining aspects of the locus and status of
community work are less well recognized. The locality orientation of community work means that it is outside the primary
structures for decision-making, which are external to the local
community. This lack of linkage to the highly centralized systems
of influence means that community work has a very low potential
as a force for change.

The avoidance of politics is part of the community development ideology, with its emphasis on consensus and harmony
of interests. This tendency is reinforced by the direct or indirect sponsorship of government, which often leads to conflict
avoidance at the expense of salience. This is particularly evident in Israel, where the community work values of localism, participatory democracy, and an apolitical style strain against a
paternalistic system of democratic centralism in which political
criteria prevail over professional values. As a result, community workers often lack appropriate resources for influencing the
bureaucracies that control the jobs, housing, medical care, education, and financial assistance needed by their clientele.

The Future of Community Work

The future of community work in these two countries is
much more circumscribed than is generally recognized. In Israel,
the constraints of the cultural barriers, professional ideology,
the locus and status of community work within politicized, centralized bureaucracies, and the organizational interests of its
sponsors appear to limit significantly any effort to develop
continuing, autonomous, self-help groups that could change their
living conditions and increase their social competence.

Similarly, in Holland, the priority assigned to inter-
organizational work, the dependent linkage of community work to
the structure of _verzuiling_ and the subsidy policies of the government, the declining significance of locality, and the absence
of an appropriate civic culture tend to confine community development to marginal forms of social brokerage.

In both countries, the environment seems more hospitable
to forms of group work and administrative involvement than to
substantive participation as envisioned in authentic community
development. In this sense, community development with its emphasis on participatory democracy is somewhat of a "foreign" and
imported ideology in Holland and Israel.

The potential for community work in Israel is related to
the possibility of there being more versatile strategies available, and this, in turn, is dependent on the likelihood of obtaining alternative, nongovernmental sponsors. The future of community

work is also related to the prospects for a "loosening" of the political system, which might result in more openness and a de-centralization of authority which would make locality-based citizen interest groups more feasible. However, there are some inherent risks in a more politicized form of community development which might strain the delicate social fabric in Israel.

In Holland, the extent to which de-pillarization and modification of the subsidy policy is continued will determine the future of community work. As presently conceived, structured, and provisioned, community work in Holland can only be applied to very minor issues, and cannot be much of a force for change in democratizing Dutch society or modifying social relationships and institutional policies and practices. At best, it can be another mild secularizing and modernizing influence in the rural areas, a minor form of community education in a highly stratified, insti-tutionalized, and centralized social system. To have even a modest impact on community structure and function, the program would re-quire (1) a clarification of objectives; (2) a cadre of adequately trained, committed and skilled personnel who have a more versatile professional ideology, and (3) organizational sponsors with a greater degree of autonomy. It would also have to generate suf-ficient incentives for effective citizen participation, help nur-ture a more receptive civic culture, and obtain the appropriate resources for influence that would be necessary. At this point, the Dutch community work program appears to lack what is needed for such tasks.

In both countries the basic question is the extent to which new, voluntary, independent, locality-based interest groups can be developed under direct or indirect governmental sponsor-ship in highly stratified societies with centralized decision-making structures and which lack a tradition for democratic cit-izen participation.

Chapter VIII

IMPLICATIONS FOR THE THEORY AND PRACTICE
OF COMMUNITY DEVELOPMENT[1]

This cross-cultural study of community development has
revealed some of the basic assumptions and determinants of CD,
and in so doing, may have contributed to a more objective evaluation of its possibilities. Because CD is conceived variously as
a program, method, movement, approach, or process, there is no
single, generally recognized or universally suitable conceptual
framework. When it is defined as a _method_, the professional
change agent is usually regarded as an enabling, rather autonomous, technical assistant interacting with a client system whose
"felt needs" generate the relatively freely chosen goals of the
study-action process within a democratic framework of values.
This model fails to make explicit the other major determinants
of practice, such as the sponsor and the sociopolitical context,
their structural interrelationships, and the specific ways in
which they can influence the goals, methods, professional roles,
obstacles, and outcomes of CD.

In this study CD has been regarded as a method, but it
has been analyzed more specifically as a form of professional
practice or as a change technology utilized by agents who are employed by a sponsoring organization to engage certain client systems within a distinctive civic culture and sociopolitical context
for community decision-making. These variables are part of the
original schema, depicted on page 2, that has served as the conceptual framework for this comparative analysis. The utility of
this framework for further research and as a guide in sensitizing
practitioners may be suggested by a discussion of how the following may affect and constrain practice: (1) sponsorship, (2) the
professionals and their ideology, and (3) the civic culture. Because of the exploratory nature of this study, the generalizations
should be regarded more as hypotheses to be tested than as propositions to be accepted.

---

[1]While it may be somewhat confusing at this point, the term
Community Development (CD) will be used in this concluding section rather than community work, since despite its ambiguity,
it is still the most frequently utilized designation.

Sponsorship

It is remarkable that the role of the sponsor has been so
neglected in the voluminous literature on CD, and that even today,
with the emergence of more self-critical attitudes, there is still
relatively little discussion of the organization responsible for
initiating a change effort.[2] The CD mystique seems to obscure
the role of the sponsoring organization. It is usually regarded
as a given and not as a variable in the total situation. As a
result, the possibility of conflict and strain between bureaucratic, professional, and client-system goals is neglected, thus
heightening the possibility for unrealistic expectations and possible deception of self and others. Since most of the sponsors
of CD are part of the national government, it would be difficult
to conceive of a more likely influence on practice. Yet even when
the effects of government on CD have been acknowledged, it is

---

[2]Typical of the infrequent and perfunctory references to the
role of sponsorship in the CD literature are: Arthur H. Niehoff,
ed., A Casebook of Social Change (Chicago: Aldine Publishing Co.,
1966), pp. 14-15; William W. and Loureide J. Biddle, The Community Development Process (New York: Holt, Rinehart and Winston,
1965), pp. 261-262. Some awareness of the consequences of governmental auspices is found in J.A. Ponsioen, "Community Development as a Process," International Review of Community Development,
Vol. 6 (1960), pp. 29-39; and G. Stensland, "Some Prerequisites
for Community Development," ibid., pp. 81-90. An exception to
the general rule is Ward H. Goodenough, Cooperation in Change (New
York: John Wiley & Sons, 1966), pp. 303-318, 429-451. More characteristic, however, is the neglect of the role of sponsorship in
such standard works as Murray G. Ross, Community Organization:
Theory, Principles and Practice (2nd ed.; New York: Harper and
Row, 1967); T.R. Batten, Training for Community Development (London: Oxford University Press, 1962); Peter Du Sautoy, The Organization of a Community Development Program (London: Oxford Univer-
sity Press, 1962); Richard W. Poston, Democracy Speaks Many
Tongues (New York: Harper and Row, 1962), and even in such a
relatively comprehensive text as Marshall B. Clinard, Slums and
Community Development: Experiments in Self-Help (New York: The
Free Press, 1966). This underestimation of the sponsor's influence contrasts sharply with the finding of the recently completed
Community Organization Curriculum Study of the Council on Social
Work Education that "of all the dimensions which enter into prac-
tice, the one which appears to account for the greatest varia-
tion. . .is the organizational context in which the activity is
conducted" (Arnold Gurin and Robert Perlman, "An Overview of the
Community Organization Curriculum Development Project and Its
Recommendations," Journal of Education for Social Work, Vol. 5,
No. 1 [Spring 1969], p. 41).

usually in terms of the necessity for bureaucratic stability and efficiency as prerequisites rather than in terms of the constraints imposed by government sponsorship.[3]

Formally, the sponsor serves as the legitimizer of the professional and sanctions his change agent role. It provides him with a rather broad and usually ambiguous mandate with direct and implied, manifest and latent expectations, and makes available to him limited resources for influence in a particular location. The sponsor determines which community conditions will be identified as problematic (e.g., deficiencies in the fields of agriculture, health, housing, welfare, education, or leisure time) and controls in great measure how they will be defined (i.e., whether in individual or social terms). In most instances the definition of the problem is in interpersonal terms, with attention directed to the necessity of changes in attitudes and personal motivation rather than modifications in social structure or institutional policy. In this way, the sponsor influences the short- and long-range goals of CD, which in turn generate the kinds of issues considered appropriate for group action. Because of linkages with government, the issues tend to be noncontroversial and of low salience, involving small-scale incremental changes whose content and direction is in the interests of the sponsor.

There is a basic interdependence between the principal practice variables: professional orientations and organizational restrictions on methodology determine the range and content of issues so that only those issues can be selected that are amenable to the educational methods and techniques open to the professional--namely, those which are ameliorative and nonpolitical do not lead to conflict, and do not require the use of pressure tactics. At the same time, the consensual and informational strategies employed are a consequence of the relatively noncontroversial and marginal issues selected for group action, which are a reflection of the programmatic interests of the sponsor.

That the goals and issues of CD are usually those of special interests, or at least acceptable to the sponsor, and not those freely chosen by the population or even regarded by them as having a high priority, is not a new finding. The recurrent concern expressed in the CD literature about the undesirability of externally imposed goals suggests that the imposition of

---

[3]See, for example, David Brokensha and Peter Hodge, _Community Development: An Interpretation_ (San Francisco: Chandler Publishing Company, 1969), pp. 147-149. It may be that in developing countries, it is less the sponsor's strengths than his weakness that is constraining. In the more developed countries, such as Holland and Israel, the degree of centralized power residing in the sponsor is more significant.

such goals may be a fairly frequent occurrence. Of late, however, there is a growing recognition that the theory of "felt needs" may require some revision, since it may be based on fallacious assumptions regarding the nature of change in rural areas and the actual range of choice available. A recent United Nations draft document, for example, maintains that the "real" needs in the community should be discovered, defining these as needs that have "strategic significance for facilitating the development process."[4] What is overlooked is the organizational source of the definition of what is considered strategic for development. It is almost as if the sponsor's interests were illicit and should therefore be suppressed. Perhaps if the legitimacy of organizational needs and interests were accorded the same recognition as those of the client-system, there might be a more objective assessment of their relationship, an enlargement of choice for the client-system, and a lessening of the possibilities for manipulation.

Similarly, more effective outcomes might result from an explication of the various forms and purposes of participation, since there is often a striking lack of congruence between the perceptions of sponsor, professional, and clientele. Some of the leading goal orientations toward participation can be arrayed on a continuum as indicated below:

TYPES OF GOAL ORIENTATIONS TOWARD RESIDENT PARTICIPATION

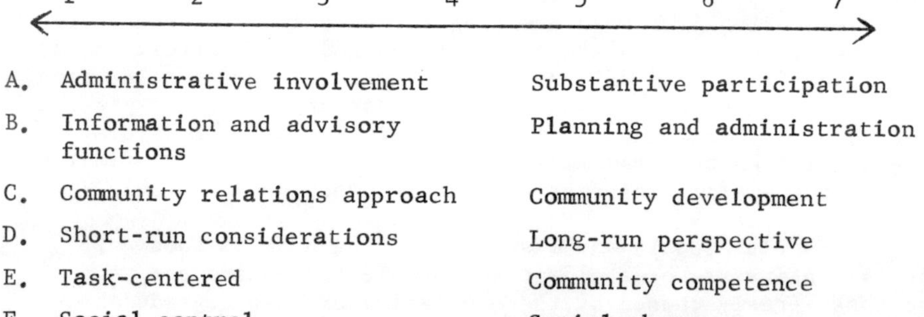

| 1 | 2 | 3 | 4 | 5 | 6 | 7 |

A. Administrative involvement   Substantive participation

B. Information and advisory   Planning and administration
functions

C. Community relations approach   Community development

D. Short-run considerations   Long-run perspective

E. Task-centered   Community competence

F. Social control   Social change

For illustrative purposes, the first dimension (A), which is based on the degree of participation, can be divided into seven types as follows:

---

[4]"Policy Issues Concerning the Future Evolution of Community Development." Unpublished draft prepared by the Regional and Community Development Staff, United Nations, April 1967 (67-47750), p. 7.

Type 1: The organization makes a plan and announces it. The community is convened for informational purposes; compliance is expected.

Type 2: The organization tries to promote a plan and seeks to develop the support which will facilitate acceptance or give sufficient sanction to the plan so that administrative compliance can be expected.

Type 3: The organization presents a plan and invites questions. It is prepared to modify the plan only if absolutely necessary.

Type 4: The organization presents a tentative plan subject to change and invites recommendations from those affected. It expects to change the plan at least slightly and perhaps even substantially.

Type 5: The organization presents a problem to the community and seeks suggestions. It hopes to join forces with the community and make joint decisions regarding the plan.

Type 6: The organization identifies and presents a problem to the community. It defines the limits of possible action and asks the community to make a series of decisions which can be embodied in a plan which it will accept.

Type 7: The organization asks the community to identify the problem and to make all of the key decisions regarding goals and means. It is willing to help the community at each step to accomplish its own goals, even to the extent of giving the community administrative control of the program.

Paralleling these modes of participation are a set of implicit purposes or functions of participation that need to be differentiated in practice, since there is some evidence that different types of participation are suitable for different goals and functions. These purposes include information, advice and consultation, support and sanction, problem identification, priority determination and goal setting, planning, policy formulation and adoption, and administration and control. Clarity regarding the organizational rationale for seeking participation not only contributes to a more meaningful compact between staff and clientele, but also helps the professional answer the fundamental questions concerning who should be involved, when, how, and for what purposes.[5]

____

[5] Among the choices to be considered in answering the question

In addition to being influenced by the sponsor's programmatic interests, which reflect its ideology, goals, and function,
the practice of CD is influenced by other organizational factors.
To begin with, the formal and informal decision-making structure
and patterns in the organization affect the character of CD. To
illustrate: Rein and Morris have proposed a series of hypotheses
describing the relationship between the authority structure of an
organization and the type of goals pursued and strategies utilized.
They claim that federated organizations such as community councils
that seek "integration" goals such as inter-agency coordination
are restricted to "cooperative rationality" or consensual strategies. On the other hand, "simple" organizations composed of like-
minded individuals committed to change goals can utilize more
versatile methods, including bargaining, lobbying, and conflict.[6]
While this hypothesis pertains more specifically to the sponsor
qua voluntary association, as in Holland or the United States, it
may also be relevant to the neighborhood and project committees
organized by the community worker, which often take on the character of a sponsor.

A similar organizational distinction pertains to the consequences of professional accountability: to a bureaucratic
authority (as in Israel) or to the policy-making board of a civic
association (such as the planning councils or neighborhood centers
in Holland). In the latter case, the number of persons whose support and understanding is necessary is much greater. This may
account for the Dutch community workers' belief that the members
of their boards of directors do not know or appreciate what they
are doing, as well as their opinion that certain actions are inhibited because they might adversely affect the relationships
among the institutional representatives on the boards. The relationship between professional autonomy and the character of the
decision-making structure is unclear, although worker autonomy
seems to vary directly with the distance from the sponsor's
decision-making center, as evidenced in the provincial development
council staff in Holland, where those assigned to regional councils exhibited the greatest degree of autonomy.

The resource base of the sponsor is another powerful
factor which can circumscribe the choice of target systems and

---

of who should be involved are the following: all members, the
most capable, most interested, most articulate, most deprived,
most influential, most representative (selected or elected),
"the leaders," or simply anyone.

[6] Martin Rein and Robert Morris, "Goals, Structures, and Strategies for Community Change," Social Work Practice, 1962 (New York:
Columbia University Press, 1962), pp. 127-145.

the issues around which people can be organized. This was seen with particular clarity in Holland, where the government's subsidy policy functioned both as a source of CD goals and as a form of dependency, since it militated against actions which might offend the sponsors. In general, exclusive reliance on tax funds for support significantly limits the issues and methods utilized by CD workers. A corollary to this is that the more routinized and relatively independent of a constituency an agent's fund-raising base is, the less likely the staff is to consult with and involve the constituency systematically in decision-making.[7]

There are other aspects of the external relationships of the sponsor that affect practice. Zald has hypothesized that where an agency is heavily dependent on its constituency, it is likely to develop a set of goals and policies and a constitution that provide little room for professional discretion.[8] This proposition seems applicable to inter-organizational work in Holland, where the sponsors are deeply enmeshed in the network of verzuiling and the involvement of this structure is a cardinal professional task. Other dimensions of the sponsors' external relations are involved in jurisdictional disputes in local communities, and in competition between national agencies in both Holland and Israel.

The public image of the sponsor also has to be taken into account, but it has been authoritatively stated that "fortunately, this is the least significant of the personal image variables."[9] In Israel, for example, the stigmas attached to government charities, as in the Ministry of Social Welfare, and to a public landlord such as Amidar were obstacles to participation that had to be overcome. The sponsor's organizational image may be important enough so that a "representative" community group is, in reality, a highly self-selective one, consisting of those for whom the agency is acceptable, thus limiting the reliability of the group for the purposes of feedback and organizational intelligence.

Finally, there are those basic features of formal organizations such as size, degree of complexity, bureaucratization, and professionalization that condition the possibilities for CD. This study seems to support the hypothesis that the greater the extent of bureaucratization, professionalization, and specialization of interests, the more narrow will be the goals which are

---

[7] Mayer N. Zald, "Organizations as Polities: An Analysis of Community Organization Agencies," *Social Work*, Vol. 11, No. 4 (October 1966), p. 60.

[8] *Ibid*.

[9] Niehoff, p. 14.

tolerated for community work. This proposition, together with others advanced earlier, strongly indicates the need for a sociology of the bureaucratic organizations that typically sponsor CD.[10] Research should be conducted to determine if specific organizational attributes of the sponsor are associated with particular types and outcomes of CD. Also helpful to both scholars and practitioners would be studies of the ways in which citizen participation may function as a "bureaucratic ideology," aiding formal organizations to accomplish their goals, with differing consequences for various target groups and clientele.[11]

Professionalism

Two observations can be made about community workers as a cadre which set them apart from other professionals. First is the relative absence of the role strain that social science theory would predict between professionals and the bureaucracies that employ them. There are at least two explanations for this phenomenon. One is that the workers enjoy a high degree of autonomy which stems from their somewhat diffuse but functional mandate; hence, there is considerable compatibility between the professional and his sponsor because there are relatively few restrictions on the professional's freedom. However, where the community workers seek to promote social action goals, there might be a noticeable strain.

Another view is that there is considerable congruence between the professional ideology of CD as espoused by the staff and the organizational interests and values of the sponsor. Both sanction only consensual, educational methods and the avoidance of conflict. Both are committed to gradualism, localism, and selective citizen involvement. Thus, as a result of the type of

---

[10]In addition to Zald, see Irving A. Spergel, _Community Problem Solving: The Delinquency Example_ (Chicago: University of Chicago Press, 1969), pp. 22-31, on the organizational character of the sponsors of community work. The effects on practice of the organizational structure of the sponsor are also discussed in S.N. Dubey, "Organizational Tension in the Community Development Blocks of India," _Human Organization_, Vol. 28, No. 1 (Spring 1969), pp. 64-71, and K.N. Singh and B.K. Singh, "Analysis of Community Development Administration at Village, Block and District Levels," _Journal of Local Administration Overseas_, Vol. 4, No. 2 (1965), pp. 99-108.

[11]An example of such a study is Elliot A. Krause, "Functions of a Bureaucratic Ideology: 'Citizen Participation,'" _Social Problems_, Vol. 16, No. 3 (Fall 1968), pp. 130-143.

issues selected and strategies employed, there is a built-in tendency to minimize any possible strain between sponsor and staff. This is reinforced "positively" by the strong identification of many staff members with national values, as well as "negatively" by the limited number of employment opportunities outside government for CD workers.

A second characteristic of the staff which sets them apart is that, at best, their professionalism is of a low order, due to their lack of common educational preparation and their recent, precarious legitimation which does not give them a monopoly over CD processes. Because the scope, content, and methods of CD so closely reflect the programmatic interests of its sponsors, it may be preferable to conceive of many community workers less as professionals and more as functional bureaucrats engaged in various forms of agency-community relations, and as seeking administrative involvement rather than the substantive participation associated with CD. Other more appropriate role models may be those of group or case workers on a micro-community level. Because of its apolitical character and dependency on sponsors, CD may also lack the versatility to which a professional practice should aspire.

Further studies of the role behavior of community workers in different organizational settings as they cope with recurrent problems would contribute to theories of professionalization, bureaucratization, and planned change.

The Civic Culture

The third major set of determinants of CD is the interplay between the attributes of the clientele and the sociopolitical context of community decision-making--i.e., the civic culture, which is a set of socially patterned expectations regarding the community problem-solving behavior of individuals in organized groups.[12] The concept of a civic culture is of particular significance in any consideration of CD as a social process aimed at achieving political socialization goals. These objectives are implicit in the somewhat hortatory claims found in Holland and in Israel to "democratize" the society by creating new, voluntary associations to serve as linkages between the citizens and their government. Similar notions are imbedded in many of the psychosocial process goals of CD, in which the acquisition of democratic

---

[12]This usage is somewhat modified from the original concept found in Gabriel A. Almond and Sidney Verba, The Civic Culture: Political Attitudes and Democracy in Five Nations (Boston: Little, Brown & Co., 1965), pp. 1-35.

participation skills become virtual ends in themselves.[13] For
such goals to be realized, it would appear that either the participants should have a self-image of themselves more as participants
and less as subjects, or CD should be capable of developing a
sense of civic efficacy in a society that would sanction it.

It is not always clear whether a social structure conducive to citizen participation is a _prerequisite_ or a _goal_ of CD,
an end or a means. This ambiguity may stem from the utopian
character of the CD ideology, in which "guides for action are
formulated from a theory of what the world ought to be and proceed
as if the world is what it ought to be."[14] In many ways, CD seems
to presuppose a participant civic culture, i.e., a set of community conditions which encourage an active citizen role and the
formation and maintenance of an infrastructure of independent,
voluntary interest groups and associations. Yet, as revealed in
this study, CD in Holland seeks to organize a clientele within a
social structure which lacks a tradition for this type of citizen
participation, and which is under the bureaucratic auspices of
and within a political system that does not encourage it. Perhaps
the character of CD in Holland is partially explained by the fact
that it assumes a civic culture and purports to be a social movement, while it is in fact organized from the top down by a governmental bureaucracy.

The values of this participant culture are not widely
shared; they are, instead, a product of the unique American and
possibly British historical experience. While other countries
may stress the legal forms and structures of a democratic polity
(e.g., "people's democracy," "democratic socialism"), they lack
a congruent civic culture which expresses a distinctive pattern
of political socialization in family, friendship, school, neighborhood, and religious and work groups, and which sanctions citizen involvement and legitimizes the sociopolitical roles of
autonomous voluntary associations.[15] For example, as Almond and

---

[13]Representative of this emphasis on process goals are the fol-
lowing: Brokensha and Hodge; Coolie Verner, "The Community De-
velopment Process," _Community Development Review_, Vol. 6, No. 1
(March 1961), pp. 49-58; Carl C. Taylor, "Community Development
Programs and Methods," _Community Development Review_, Vol. 3
(December 1956), pp. 34-42; and J.D. Mezirow, "Community Develop-
ment as an Educational Process," _International Review of Community
Development_, Vol. 5 (1960), pp. 137-150.

[14]Rein and Morris, "Emerging Patterns in Community Planning,"
Social Work Practice, 1963 (New York: Columbia University Press,
1963), p. 66.

[15]Almond and Verba, pp. 266-306; Jack Dennis _et al._, "Political

Verba have shown in their classic study of five countries, only
in the United States is there a strong belief in the effectiveness
of group action and a propensity to enlist the aid of others in
informal groups.[16] It is generally acknowledged that no other
country has the enormous network of voluntary associations and
interest groups that exists in the United States. There is additional evidence in other comparative political research which
indicates wide differences in political behavior and supports
the proposition that the civic values and norms which are generally presumed in CD are rooted in a specific national culture.[17]
As Brokensha and Hodge put it in their critique of the political
implications of CD, "In the field of CD the assumption that all societies are, at least latently, democratic is one of the greatest
sources of misunderstanding."[18]

It may well be that the ideology of CD represents an
instance of cultural diffusion of a set of American values that

---

Socialization to Democratic Orientations in Four Western Systems,"
Political Studies, Vol. 1, No. 1 (1968), pp. 71-101; and Donald B.
Searing, "The Comparative Study of Elite Socialization," *Comparative Political Studies*, Vol. 1, No. 4 (January 1969), pp. 471-
500.

[16]Almond and Verba, pp. 150-159. A provocative reanalysis of
some of this comparative data points up some of the political
implications of lower-class organizations. See Norman H. Nie,
G. Bingham Powell, Jr., and Kenneth Prewitt, "Social Structure
and Political Participation: Developmental Relationships, II,"
American Political Science Review, Vol. 63 (September 1969), pp.
808-832.

[17]Additional examples of this research can be found in the
series of articles in the *International Social Science Journal*,
Vol. 12, No. 1 (1960), pp. 7-99. The Western bias of professional ideologies is discussed by Jan F. DeJongh, "Western Social
Work and the Afro-Asian World," *Social Service Review*, Vol. 43,
No. 1 (March 1969), pp. 50-58, and John Friedmann, "Intention
and Reality: The American Planner Overseas," *Journal of the
American Institute of Planners*, Vol. 35, No. 3 (May 1969), pp.
187-194. The absence of the cultural and social prerequisites
for citizen participation in Western Germany is discussed in R.
Vogel and P. Oel, *Gemeinde und Gemeinschaftshadeln: Zur Analyse
der Bedriffe, Community Organization und Community Development*
(Stuttgart: W. Kohlhammer Verlag, 1966). Appreciation is extended to my student Peter Nimmermann for calling this last reference to my attention.

[18]Brokensha and Hodge, p. 165.

are imperfectly realized in the United States and, ironically, about which there is growing disillusionment. The latter is evident in the doubts about the validity and feasibility of local initiative in the form of neighborhood-based problem-solving groups. On the one hand, it has been claimed by some that the proliferation of such groups in recent years in most cities has virtually stalemated the community decision-making process because so many competing interests are now articulated that the prevailing influence structure is incapable of resolving the conflicts.[19] Apart from asserting its potential sociotherapeutic benefits, other studies of neighborhood participation have concluded that it has a negligible impact on policy because most decisions affecting residents are no longer left to the market, but are highly politicized and are made on a much higher level than the neighborhood. In addition to showing this lack of extra-community linkages, and the inability of locality-based groups to form coalitions, recent analyses of participation by low-income citizens have shown that they are highly dependent on outside sponsorship and resources, and generally lack the capability of implementing plans.[20]

If, however, CD regards the nurturing of citizen participation as a _goal_ rather than as a prerequisite, then its credentials and resources as a social movement deserve a more careful assessment. To what extent can CD be a force for political

---

[19]The paradox that an increase in participation may create a sense of powerlessness and consequent frustration is perceptively discussed in Daniel Bell and Virginia Held, "The Community Revolution," _The Public Interest_, No. 16 (Summer 1969), pp. 142-179. Some empirical support for this belief is found in Robert L. Crain and Donald B. Rosenthal, "Community Status as a Dimension of Local Decision-Making" in Hans B.C. Spiegel, ed., _Citizen Participation in Urban Development_, Selected Readings Series Eight, Vol. 1, Concepts and Issues (Washington, D.C., NTL Institute for Applied Behavioral Science, 1968), pp. 241-270.

[20]Evidence supporting these conclusions regarding citizen participation in low-income neighborhoods can be found in John B. Turner, ed., _Neighborhood Organization and Community Action_ (New York: National Association of Social Workers, 1968); Arnold Gurin and Joan Ecklein, "Community Organization For What? Political Power or Service Delivery," _Social Work Practice, 1968_ (New York: Columbia University Press, 1968), pp. 1-15; Ralph M. Kramer, _Participation of the Poor: Comparative Community Case Studies in the War on Poverty_ (Englewood Cliffs: Prentice-Hall, Inc., 1969); David M. Austin, "Organizing for Neighborhood Improvement or Social Change" (unpublished Ph.D. dissertation, Brandeis University, February 1969).

socialization and the eventual development of a participant culture? An objective evaluation of CD's potential for these tasks suggests that while it may make a modest contribution to political socialization, it lacks the necessary goals and opposition to generate the appropriate degree of solidarity, types of leadership, organizational structures, and strategies associated with a social movement. The character of its governmental sponsorship and professional cadres marks it as primarily a force for social stability and control--for system maintenance, not institutional change. Although it may assume, require, or aspire to an activist political culture, in practice, as we have seen, CD avoids controversy, opposition, and interaction with the political system. Its strains are similar to those found among economic planners in the developing nations:

> The planner in these nations has a role that derives
> from another economic and cultural system and must be
> fulfilled in a society lacking the prerequisites for
> its integration. The role itself cannot be understood
> in conventional bureaucratic terms; it must be seen as
> implying a claim to political power through its vaunted
> ability to guide choices for desired future stakes.
> Such knowledge has an anti-political base, and thus
> contributes to an anti-political ideology.[21]

In addition, its locus, low status, and lack of power are serious obstacles to a more effective sociopolitical role for CD. As the evidence in this study shows, CD has had virtually no impact on the structural changes occurring in Holland and Israel. Finally, a strong argument has been made that civic participation can be more effectively promoted by economic development, with its increasing division of labor, rising middle class, and political organization of the peasantry for land reform, than by means of planned CD efforts aimed at cooperative relations.[22]

In addition to its assumption or goal of citizen participation and its pro-Western bias, other basic CD concepts are being reevaluated. These include long-standing beliefs regarding (1) felt needs, (2) self-help, (3) local initiative, and (4) gradualism, in addition to some questions about the transferability

------

[21]Warren F. Ilchman, Alice Stone Ilchman, and Philip K. Hastings, The New Men of Knowledge and the Developing Nations (Berkeley: University of California, Institute of Governmental Studies, June 1968), p. 66.

[22]Charles J. Erasmus, "Community Development and the 'Encogido' Syndrome," Human Organization, Vol. 27, No. 1 (Spring 1968), pp. 65-74.

of the principles and methods of rural CD to urban communities in advanced, developing countries.

(1) A recent United Nations document notes that "some restatement is required" of the theory of felt needs since these are not fixed but are now seen as the product of a culture and socioeconomic situation, and are likely to change as the latter are modified.[23] Furthermore, the document continues, it is increasingly recognized that the felt needs of a local community may not be compatible with those of other communities, particularly from a national perspective. Community workers are urged to discover "real" needs, i.e., those considered strategic for development, although it is not clear how this new criterion avoids the imposition of organizational and professional definitions which community workers have always been urged to avoid. That this advice may seldom be needed is suggested by a comprehensive survey of CD workers in which less than 13 percent mentioned "meeting the felt needs of the people" as a strategy.[24]

(2) There is increased awareness that self-help is less than an all-inclusive, all-purpose strategy, and that without structural changes in the economy or in the political system, expectations of self-help are unrealistic. In practice, CD characteristically avoids the systemic and structural forces that perpetuate the major problematic conditions affecting the population, such as poverty, unemployment, poor housing, inadequate medical care and education--few of which are amenable to self-help strategies.[25] In this way, CD becomes a way of avoiding necessary changes in social policy. It can also be accused of being diversionary by trivializing the collective efforts of the people.

(3) The locality orientation of CD and reliance on primary group, face-to-face cooperation is regarded by some critics as anachronistic, since most of the problems which vitally affect an increasingly mobile population are not amenable to solutions

---

[23] See footnote 4 above.

[24] Herbert H. Hyman, Gene N. Levine, and Charles R. Wright, _Methods to Induce Change at the Local Level: An International Survey of Expert Advice_ (Geneva: United Nations Research Institute for Social Development, 1967), pp. 85-86.

[25] This point is stressed in S.K. Khinduka, "Community Development: Its Potentials and Limitations," _Social Work Practice, 1969_ (New York: Columbia University Press, 1969), pp. 15-28, and Erasmus. Both of these studies are also critical of the locality orientation and the gradualism of CD as described in this study.

at this level. Largely because of this, CD is usually confined
to noncontroversial and peripheral issues. It often fails to
produce substantive results and avoids evaluation. Frequently,
when the ineffectiveness of CD is pointed out, refuge is taken
in the assertion that its goals are intangible. On the other
hand, where there have been tangible accomplishments, they have
usually been attained at the expense of procedural aspects. Finally, in those rare instances where self-sustaining, cooperative
relationships have survived the departure of the change agent,
such intensive skilled work has been required that they do not
constitute a realistic basis for widespread application. It is
ironic, as Charles Erasmus has remarked, that the goals and pro-
cedures of CD have resulted in an effective international movement that is apparently ineffectual on the community level.[26]

(4) Finally, the intrinsic gradualism of CD is regarded
as an extremely limited, "soft," or "gentlemanly" approach to
change in the face of a widening gap between the classes and the
highly intractable, vested interests which oppose any social
change. CD has also been criticized because of its assumption
that attitudinal change is a pre-condition of social change, and
for concentrating attention on the values and belief systems of
the victims and not on those of the decision-makers. In its
emphasis on individual psychosocial change and on sociotherapy,
CD, it is asserted, tends to institutionalize the status quo,
and in many respects may actually be dysfunctional to a process
of modernization.

While this indictment refers principally to rural CD, most
of it also applies to urban community work in the more developed
countries to which the dominant features of CD have been transferred, i.e., where the basic unit of practice is a small disadvantaged area and where there is a reliance on consensual, self-
help strategies. The origin of the CD ideology in rural and small
town life results in a poor cultural fit in urban areas, where
the community environment is so much more complex, disorderly, and
dynamic. The lack of agreement on values and urban goals, the
multiplicity of competing interests, and the dispersion of influence raise serious questions regarding the possibilities of CD
as a problem-solving process.[27] These vexing social conditions

---

[26]Erasmus, p. 66.

[27]Daniel J. Scher, "The Role of the University in Community
Development: An Examination of Three Concepts," School of Social
and Community Services and the University Extension Division,
University of Missouri, Columbia, January 1969. An optimistic
view of the possibilities for urban community development can be
found in Clinard.

are usually cited as justifying the need for urban CD, but data supporting this claim are hard to come by due to the paucity of evaluative research.[28] Yet there seems to be some evidence, even if much of it is impressionistic, to draw upon in attempting to answer the questions: What should be the boundaries of CD? What is it capable of?

While recognizing that it is no substitute for planned institutional change, CD has been urged to incorporate social action goals, roles, and strategies popularized in the United States in the war on poverty and to deemphasize the enabling process and self-help model.[29] This assumes an enormous versatility on the part of CD, which at least in Holland and Israel has not been demonstrated, i.e., the capacity to develop new, autonomous, self-perpetuating, locality-based groups. Nor is there much evidence that citizen groups organized around their own social service needs move on to more politicized issues. Experience suggests that different organizational structures and membership composition may be required. Furthermore, such a prescription overlooks the important constraints imposed on the more politicized forms of CD by its sponsors, apart from other disabilities to which such groups are prone even when there is an appropriate civic culture. So far, then, there is an insufficient foundation in theory or in successful practice to expect a viable union between the usual forms of community development and social action.

Instead of seeking to combine educational and political goals or to assume that the same group can move from the former to the latter, some Dutch social scientists have recommended separation of the sociopedagogic and the sociopolitical into two distinct forms of practice.[30] Implicit in this differentiation

---

[28] A content assessment of 945 articles in the CD literature revealed that over half were devoted to the ideals and philosophy of the movement, less than a third were reports of specific projects (usually by those directly responsible), and only 18 percent qualified in any way as analytical papers. There were "few rigorous project studies or critical analyses to show how the doctrine works in practice" (Erasmus).

[29] Khinduka.

[30] This distinction is embodied in the concept of _androgogie,_ the adult counterpart of sociopedagogy as found in the work of T.T. ten Have. See his _De Wetenschap der Sociale Agogie_ (Groningen, 1962) and M. Van Beugen, _Sociale Technologie_ (Assen: van Gorum & Co., 1968). A somewhat contrary argument in favor of combining integration and planning goals is found in David Popenoe, "Community Development and Community Planning," _Journal_

is a recognition of the contrast between the goals of changing
individuals and those of changing systems. Along with this distinction, there may be a division of labor, with CD assigned to
the rural areas and inter-organizational work for urban areas.
Separation of the educational and the political or social change
goals has the apparent virtue of greater consistency and clarity,
and points to a conception of CD whereby it is primarily a form
of group work or adult education with a much less pretentious
function. The appropriate tasks, professional skills, and evaluative criteria for these more limited educational goals still have
to be explicated, however. This means that CD would have to specify its process goals rather than take refuge in them to explain
failures in task accomplishment. Two benefits of this approach
would be an increased possibility for evaluation and a greater
degree of congruence between ideology and practice. Sociopedagogic or educational processes do not, however, occur in a vacuum;
people learn through specific tasks, and if these are trivial or
highly controversial, then certain outcomes must be expected.
For example, it does not seem possible, if CD is going to deal
with salient issues, that it can avoid politics; therefore, it
will have to confront the serious constraints that have previously been noted. Under these circumstances, it may seem that CD
can live neither with nor without politics.

This dilemma is only one that stems from the diverse competing goals contained within the CD ideology, such as task/pro-
cess, educational/political, individual/social. Because of this
diversity and strain, it is difficult to conceive of only one
practice model, and yet this has generally been the case despite
a series of sporadic and early efforts to formulate various types
of CD. For example, Ross in 1955 identified three forms of CD:
external implantation, multiple impact, and inner resources.[31]
Tumin in 1958 found eight different dimensions along which CD
varied: (1) the size of the unit, (2) the scope of the program,
(3) the nature of the developer (public or private), (4) the time
perspective, (5) variation in goal orientations, (6) balance of
"welfare vs. science," (7) balance of local vs. external sources
employed in the project, and (8) concern for follow-up.[32] Using
five similar variables, Eaton in 1963 proposed three ideological

---

of the American Institute of Planners, Vol. 33, No. 4 (July 1967),
pp. 259-265. See also G.V. Haigh, "Competing Strategies for the
Community Development Function in the Peace Corps," International
Review of Community Development, Vol. 12 (1963), pp. 53-66.

[31]Ross, pp. 7-17.

[32]Melvin M. Tumin, "Some Social Requirements for Effective Community Development," Community Development Review, No. 11 (December 1958), pp. 1-39.

models: Social Darwinist, expert, and mutualistic.[33] More recently, Rothman has grouped together twelve conceptions of problem, community, clientele, professional role, etc., into a three-fold scheme of practice: locality (community) development, social planning, and social action.[34] The author of this work, drawing on some empirical studies of the participation of the poor in poverty programs, has modified Warren's trichotomy of community conflict resolution based on anticipated degree of agreement and has delineated the respective goals, methods, strategies, and resources for influence for debates, games, and fights.[35] Similarly, Cleland has identified four types of planned change efforts based on the extent of shared decision-making and scope of change: directed, planned, guided, and developmental.[36] Finally, Spergel, in one of the few comprehensive frameworks for practice, defines two strategies--social stability and social change--and relates them to distinctive professional role behaviors in the seven phases of community problem-solving.[37]

What is the significance of these initial efforts at theory building? Because of the different orientations toward CD and the multiplicity of goals and functions, greater conceptual clarity is required to guide further practice and research. The first step in clearing the "conceptual jungle which is the intellectual habitat of CD and community action"[38] might be one of separating out and defining as ideal types the basic forms of CD in terms of major practice variables. The next stage could consist of the empirical testing of these definitional propositions to see if in reality they cluster together in the predicted fashion. For example, there might be an investigation to determine under which of the following conditions a CD process occurs most often: a high degree of interest congruence, diffused

---

[33]Joseph Eaton, "Community Development Ideologies," Community Development Review, Vol. 11 (1963), pp. 37-50.

[34]Jack Rothman, "Three Models of Community Organization Practice," Social Work Practice, 1968 (New York: Columbia University Press, 1968), pp. 16-47.

[35]Kramer, p. 184.

[36]Courtney B. Cleland, "A Typology of Purposive Social Change for Community Action and Community Development," expanded version of a paper presented at the Pacific Sociological Association meeting, March 31, 1967, Long Beach, California.

[37]Spergel, pp. 3-152.

[38]Cleland, p. 15.

pattern of power distribution, low potential for coalition formation, small community size, voluntary auspices, or support of
key leadership and integration goals.[39] The relationships among
the practice variables in the schema used in this study, such as
the types of sponsors, goals, issues, and methods, can also be a
source of hypotheses to be tested which may yield sensitizing
concepts and guidelines for professionals.

Formidable research obstacles are presented by these concepts, however, because they involve complex problems of multi-
variate analysis in which phenomena vary independently as well as
in conjunction with each other. While there are other approaches
to the development of practice theory that should be pursued,[40]
the delineation of typologies as a first step has considerable
utility. Classification can help professionals clarify their
goals and purposes, orient them to the type of planned change
they are seeking, and draw their attention to the basic assumptions and prerequisites underlying the practice of CD.

---

[39] These variables are suggested by the study reported by Roland
L. Warren and Herbert H. Hyman, "Purposive Community Change in
Consensus and Dissensus Situations," Community Mental Health
Journal, Vol. 2, No. 4 (Winter 1967), pp. 293-300.

[40] Gurin and Perlman, pp. 37-48.

GLOSSARY OF HEBREW TERMS

Amidar: Israel National Housing Corporation for Immigrants.

Egged: The national bus cooperative of the Histadrut.

Haganah: The Pre-State Defense Forces of Israel.

Histadrut: The General Federation of Labor.

Jewish Agency: Originally organized under the British Mandate
        for Palestine as the official body to aid in the estab-
        lishment of the Jewish National Home; promotes immigrant
        resettlement, agricultural colonization, and various cul-
        tural and educational programs.

Knesset: The National Parliament of Israel.

Kupat Cholim: "Sick Fund," the health insurance and medical
        care programs of the Histadrut.

Mitzvah: A meritorious deed or duty required by religious law.

Moadon: A community center.

Saad: Ministry of Social Welfare.

Shikun: Apartment housing unit, usually managed by Amidar.

Vaad Leumi: The National Council, the self-governing body for
        the Jewish community in Palestine under the British Man-
        date.

Yishuv: The Jewish community in Palestine under the British
        Mandate.

BIBLIOGRAPHY

Almond, Gabriel A., and Verba, Sidney. The Civic Culture: Polit-
    ical Attitudes and Democracy in Five Nations. Boston: Little,
    Brown & Co., 1965.

Ancona, Dov. "The Beth Shemesh and Netivot Demonstration Project
    as a Local Enterprise and as a Pilot Project." Jerusalem:
    Henrietta Szold Institute, National Institute for Research
    and Behavioral Sciences, August 1969.

Akzin, Benjamin, and Dror, Yehezkel. Israel: High-Pressure
    Planning. Syracuse: Syracuse University Press, 1966.

Austin, David M. "Organizing for Neighborhood Improvement or
    Social Change." Unpublished Ph.D. dissertation, Brandeis
    University, February 1969.

Avineri, Shlomo. "The Post-Ben-Gurion Era," Midstream, XI, 3
    (September 1965).

Banfield, Edward C. Political Influence. New York: The Free
    Press of Glencoe, 1961).

Bar-Yosef, R., and Schild, E.O. "Pressures and Defenses in Bureau-
    cratic Roles," The American Journal of Sociology, Vol. 61,
    No. 6 (May 1966).

Batten, T.R. Communities and Their Development. London: Oxford
    University Press, 1964.

________. Training for Community Development. London: Oxford
    University Press, 1962.

Bell, Daniel, and Held, Virginia. "The Community Revolution,"
    The Public Interest, No. 16 (Summer 1969).

Ben-David, Joseph, ed. Agricultural Planning and Village Commu-
    nity in Israel. Paris: UNESCO, 1964.

Bernstein, Marver H. The Politics of Israel: The First Decade
    of Statehood. Princeton: Princeton University Press, 1957.

Biddle, William W., and Loureide J. The Community Development
    Process. New York: Holt, Reinhart and Winston, 1965.

BIBLIOGRAPHY

Billingsley, Andrew. "Bureaucratic and Professional Orientation Patterns in Social Casework," Social Service Review, Vol. 38, No. 4 (December 1964).

Blau, Peter M., and Scott, W. Richard. Formal Organizations. San Francisco: Chandler Publishing Co., 1962.

Blum, A., Miranda, M., and Meyer, M. "Goals and Means for Social Change." In John B. Turner, ed., Neighborhood Organization for Community Action. [See "Turner."]

Boderie, H.J.H. "Special Social Policy in the Dutch Stimulation Areas." The Hague: Ministry of Cultural Affairs, Recreation and Social Welfare, 1965.

Brokensha, David, and Hodge, Peter. Community Development: An Interpretation. San Francisco: Chandler Publishing Company, 1969.

Caiden, Gerald E. "Israeli Administration after Twenty Years," Public Administration in Israel and Abroad, 1967, 8. Jerusalem, 1968.

__________. Israel's Administrative Culture. Berkeley: University of California, Institute of Governmental Studies, forthcoming.

Cantril, Hadley. The Pattern of Human Concerns. New Brunswick, N.J.: Rutgers University Press, 1965.

Cleland, Courtney B. "A Typology of Purposive Social Change for Community Action and Community Development." Expanded version of a paper presented at the Pacific Sociological Association meeting, March 31, 1967, Long Beach, California.

Clinard, Marshall B. Slums and Community Development: Experiments in Self-Help. New York: The Free Press, 1966.

Cloward, Richard A., and Pivan, Frances. "The Professional Bureaucracies: Benefit Systems as Influence Systems." In Ralph Kramer and Harry Specht, eds., Readings in Community Organization Practice. [See "Kramer."]

Cohen, Erik. "Social Images in an Israeli Development Town," Human Relations, Vol. 21, No. 2 (May 1968).

Crain, Robert L., and Rosenthal, Donald B. "Community Status as a Dimension of Local Decision-Making." In Hans B.C. Spiegel, ed., Citizen Participation in Urban Development, Selected Readings Series Eight, Vol. 1, Concepts and Issues. Washington, D.C.: NTL Institute for Applied Behavioral Science, 1968.

BIBLIOGRAPHY

Daalder, Hans. "The Netherlands: Opposition in a Segmented
     Society." In Robert Dahl, ed., *Political Opposition in
     Western Democracies*. New Haven: Yale University Press,
     1966.

__________, and Bone, Robert C. "The Dynamics of Dutch Politics,"
     Journal of Politics, Vol. XXIV, No. 1 (February 1962).

Dahl, Robert. *Who Governs*? New Haven: Yale University Press,
     1961.

De Gier, A. Interview printed in *NIMO Bulletin*, No. 2 (April
     1968). Translated by T. Hijna.

De Jong, Otto J. "Dutch Protestantism," *Delta*, Vol. 9, No. 4
     (Winter 1966-67).

De Jongh, Jan F. "Western Social Work and the Afro-Asian World,"
     Social Service Review, Vol. 43, No. 1 (March 1969).

De Lange, Daniel. "Dutch Catholicism," *Delta*, Vol. 9, No. 4
     (Winter 1966-67).

Dennis, Jack, *et al*. "Political Socialization to Democratic
     Orientations in Four Western Systems," *Political Studies*,
     Vol. 1, No. 1 (1968).

Dror, Yehezkel. "Nine Main Characteristics of Governmental
     Administration in Israel," *Public Administration in Israel
     and Abroad, 1964*, No. 5, Jerusalem, 1965.

Dubey, S.N. "Organizational Tension in the Community Development
     Blocks of India," *Human Organization*, Vol. 28, No. 1 (Spring
     1969).

Du Sautoy, Peter. *The Organization of a Community Development
     Program*. London: Oxford University Press, 1962.

Eaton, Joseph. "Community Development Ideologies," *Community
     Development Review*, Vol. 11 (1963).

Eisenstadt, S.N. *The Absorption of Immigrants*. Glencoe: Free
     Press, 1955.

__________. *Israeli Society*. New York: Basic Books, Inc., 1967.

Erasmus, Charles J. "Community Development and the 'Encogido'
     Syndrome," *Human Organization*, Vol. 27, No. 1 (Spring 1968).

Fein, Leonard J. *Politics in Israel*. Boston: Little, Brown
     and Company, 1967.

BIBLIOGRAPHY

Friedmann, Georges. *The End of the Jewish People*? Garden City: Doubleday-Anchor Books, 1968.

Friedmann, John. "Intention and Reality: The American Planner Overseas," *Journal of the American Institute of Planners*, Vol. 35, No. 3 (May 1969).

Gadourek, I., *et al*. "Involvement in Cultural Systems in The Netherlands: Its Measurement and Social Correlates," *Social Forces*, Vol. 40, No. 4 (May 1962).

Goodenough, Ward H. *Cooperation in Change*. New York: John Wiley & Sons, 1966.

Goudsblom, Johan. *Dutch Society*. New York: Random House, 1967.

Groenman, Sj. "Community Development in Urban Areas," *International Review of Community Development*, Vol. 7 (1961).

________. "Social Development on a Territorial Basis." The Netherlands Association for Social and Cultural Educational Work, n.d.

Gurin, Arnold, and Ecklein, Joan. "Community Organization for What? Political Power or Service Delivery," *Social Work Practice, 1968*. New York: Columbia University Press, 1968.

________, and Perlman, Robert. "An Overview of the Community Organization Curriculum Development Project and Its Recommendations," *Journal of Education for Social Work*, Vol. 5, No. 1 (Spring 1969).

Haigh, G.V. "Competing Strategies for the Community Development Function in the Peace Corps," *International Review of Community Development*, Vol. 12 (1963).

Hall, Peter. "A Polycentric Metropolis: Randstad Holland," *Delta*, Vol. 10, Nos 1-2 (Spring-Summer 1967).

Hendriks, G. *Community Organization: A Collection of Readings on Social Planning and Community Organization*. The Hague: Ministry for Social Work, 1964.

________. *Social Planning and Community Development*. The Hague: Ministry of Cultural Affairs, Recreation and Social Welfare, 1967.

Hodara, Joseph. "Patterns of Action for a Demonstration Program in Beit Shemesh and Netivot." Jerusalem: Henrietta Szold Institute, National Institute for Research and Behavioral Sciences, September 1967.

BIBLIOGRAPHY

Hoogerwerf, A. "Latent Socio-political Issues in The Netherlands,"
     Sociologia Neerlandica, II (1965).

Hyman, Herbert H., Levine, Gene N., and Wright, Charles R. _Methods
     to Induce Change at the Local Level: An International Survey
     of Expert Advice_. Geneva: United Nations Research Institute
     for Social Development, 1967.

Ilchman, Warren F., Ilchman, Alice Stone, and Hastings, Philip K.
     The New Men of Knowledge and the Developing Nations. Berkeley:
     University of California, Institute of Governmental Studies,
     June 1968.

International Social Science Journal, Vol. 12, No. 1 (1960).
     Various articles.

Israel, State of. Central Bureau of Statistics. "Internal Migra-
     tion," Part 1. Population and Housing Census Publication No.
     19. Jerusalem, 1965.

________. Central Office of Information, Prime Minister's Office.
     Israel Government Yearbook, 5727 (1966/67). March 1968.

________. _Israel Government Yearbook, 5728_ (1967/68). 1969.

________. The Jewish Agency, Absorption and Information Depart-
     ments. _Sixteen Years of Immigrant Absorption_. Jerusalem,
     1964.

________. Ministry of Labor, Manpower Planning Authority. "Man-
     power in Development Towns." December 1964.

________. Ministry of Social Welfare. _Report on Urban Develop-
     ment--Implications for Social Welfare_. Thirteenth Interna-
     tional Conference of Social Work, Washington 1966 (Jerusalem,
     July 1966).

________. _Social Welfare in Israel_. Jerusalem, December 1961.

Khinduka, S.K. "Community Development: Its Potentials and Limi-
     tations," _Social Work Practice, 1969_. New York: Columbia
     University Press, 1969.

Kraines, Oscar. _Government and Politics in Israel_. Boston:
     Houghton Mifflin Company, 1961.

Kramer, Ralph M. _Participation of the Poor: Comparative Commu-
     nity Case Studies in the War on Poverty_. Englewood Cliffs:
     Prentice-Hall, Inc., 1969.

BIBLIOGRAPHY

__________, and Specht, Harry, eds. Readings in Community Organization Practice. Englewood Cliffs: Prentice-Hall, Inc., 1969.

Krause, Elliot A. "Functions of a Bureaucratic Ideology: 'Citizen Participation'," Social Problems, Vol. 16, No. 3 (Fall 1968).

Levine, S., White, Paul E., and Paul, Benjamin D. "Community Inter-organizational Problems in Providing Medical Care and Social Services." In Ralph Kramer and Harry Specht, eds., Readings in Community Organization Practice. [See "Kramer."]

Lijphart, Arend. The Politics of Accommodation: Pluralism and Democracy in The Netherlands. Berkeley: University of California Press, 1968.

Lotan, Giora. "The Social Services of Israel," Public Administration in Israel and Abroad, 1964, 5, Jerusalem, 1965.

Maas-Mondig. Rotterdam Council of Social Welfare, Vol. 1, Nos. 1 and 2 (January-February 1968).

Martin, Roscoe C., et al. Decisions in Syracuse. New York: Doubleday-Anchor Books, 1965.

Matras, Judah. Social Change in Israel. Chicago: Aldine Publishing Co., 1965.

Mezirow, J.D. "Community Development as an Educational Process," International Review of Community Development, Vol. 5 (1960).

Moberg, David O. "Religion and Society in The Netherlands and in America," American Quarterly, Vol. 13, No. 2, Pt. 1 (Summer 1961).

__________. "Social Differentiation in The Netherlands," Social Forces, Vol. 29, No. 4 (May 1961).

Morlan, Robert L. "Cabinet Government at the Municipal Level in the Dutch Experience," Western Political Quarterly, Vol. 17, No. 2 (June 1964).

Netherlands, The. Ministry for Social Work. "Government Regulations on the Subsidies for Private Bodies in the Field of Social Welfare." 1962.

__________. Netherlands Government Information Service. Digest of the Kingdom of The Netherlands: Social Aspects. N.d.

Neipris, Joseph. "Social Services in Israel," International Conference of Jewish Communal Service, August 19-23, 1967, Jerusalem, Israel.

__________. "Some Origins of Social Policy in a New State: The Formation of Policy Concerning Aged Immigrants in Israel, 1948-55." Unpublished Ph.D. dissertation, University of California, School of Social Welfare, 1966.

Nie, Norman H., Powell, G. Bingham, Jr., and Prewitt, Kenneth. "Social Structure and Political Participation: Developmental Relationships, II," American Political Science Review, Vol. 63 (September 1969).

Niehoff, Arthur H., ed. A Case Book of Social Change. Chicago: Aldine Publishing Co., 1966.

Ohlin, Lloyd. "Urban Community Development." In Ralph Kramer and Harry Specht, eds., Readings in Community Organization Practice. [See "Kramer."]

Parkes, Rev. S. Haden. Window Gardens for the People and Clean and Tidy Rooms: Being an Experiment to Improve the Homes of the London Poor. London: S.W. Partridge, 1863.

Patai, Raphael. Israel Between East and West: A Study in Human Relations. Philadelphia: Jewish Publication Society, 1953.

Peper, Bram. "Afbraak van het Opbouwwerk? Een Beleidssociologische Kritiek," Mens en Maatschappij, Vol. 44, No. 2 (March/April 1969).

Petersen, William. "Fertility Trends and Population Policy: Some Comments on the Van Heek-Hofstee Debate," Sociologia Neerlandica, Vol. III, No. II (1966).

Polsby, Nelson W. Community Power and Political Theory. New Haven: Yale University Press, 1963.

Ponsioen, J.A. "Community Development as a Process," International Review of Community Development, Vol. 6 (1960).

Popenoe, David. "Community Development and Community Planning," Journal of the American Institute of Planners, Vol. 23, No. 4 (July 1967).

Poston, Richard W. Democracy Speaks Many Tongues. New York: Harper and Row, 1962.

Reid, William J. "Inter-organizational Coordination in Social Welfare: A Theoretical Approach to Analysis and Intervention." In Ralph Kramer and Harry Specht, eds., Readings in Community Organization Practice. [See "Kramer."]

Rein, Martin, and Morris, Robert. "Emerging Patterns in Community

Planning," _Social Work Practice, 1963_. New York: Columbia University Press, 1963.

________. "Goals, Structures and Strategies for Community Change," _Social Work Practice, 1962_. New York: Columbia University Press, 1962. Also in Ralph Kramer and Harry Specht, eds., _Readings in Community Organization Practice_. [See "Kramer."]

Reinders, Jacob E. "The Netherlands Development Areas Reach a New Phase," _Community Development Journal_, No. 5 (January 1967).

Reissman, Leonard. "A Study of Role Conceptions in Bureaucracy," Social Forces, 27, No. 3 (March 1949).

Ross, Murray G., and Lappin, B.W. _Community Organization: Theory, Principles, and Practice_. 2nd ed.; New York: Harper and Row, 1967.

Rossi, Peter H. "Community Decision Making," _Administrative Science Quarterly_, Vol. 1, No. 4 (March 1957).

Rothman, Jack. "Three Models of Community Organization Practice," _Social Work Practice, 1968_. New York: Columbia University Press, 1968.

Schaafsma, Henk. "Mirror of a Pillarized Society: Broadcasting in The Netherlands," _Delta_, Vol. 9, No. 4 (Winter 1966-67).

Scher, Daniel J. "The Role of the University in Community Development: An Examination of Three Concepts." School of Social and Community Services and the University Extension Division, University of Missouri, Columbia, January 1969.

Scott, W. Richard. "Professionals in Bureaucracies--Areas of Conflict." In Howard M. Vollmer and Donald L. Mills, eds., _Professionalization_. Englewood Cliffs: Prentice-Hall, Inc., 1966.

Searing, Donald B. "The Comparative Study of Elite Socialization," _Comparative Political Studies_, Vol. 1, No. 4 (January 1969).

Seker Avodim Kehilatim B'yisrael. Jerusalem: Keren Giora Yoseftal, May 1969.

Selzer, Michael. _The Aryanization of the Jewish State_. New York: David White Co., 1967.

________. _The Outcasts of Israel: Communal Tensions in the Jewish State_. Jerusalem: The Council of the Sephardi Community, 1965).

BIBLIOGRAPHY

Selznick, Philip. _TVA and the Grass Roots: A Study in the Sociology of Formal Organization_. New York: Harper and Row, 1966.

Shuval, Judith P. "Emerging Patterns of Ethnic Strain in Israel," _Social Forces_, Vol. XL, No. 4 (1962).

________. _Immigrants on the Threshold_. New York: Atherton Press, 1963.

Silver, Harold. "Developments in Ministry of Social Welfare." Report on Second Year of Consultantship, May 1965. [Mimeograph]

Singh, K.N. and Singh, B.K. "Analysis of Community Development Administration at Village, Block and District Levels," _Journal of Local Administration Overseas_, Vol. 4, No. 2 (1965).

Smilansky, Moshe, _et al_., eds. _Child and Youth Welfare in Israel_. Jerusalem: Henrietta Szold Institute for Child and Youth Welfare, 1960.

Spergel, Irving A. _Community Problem Solving: The Delinquency Example_. Chicago: University of Chicago Press, 1969.

Spiegel, Erika. _New Towns in Israel: Urban and Regional Planning and Development_. Stuttgart/Bern: Karl Kramer Verlag, 1966.

Stensland, G. "Some Prerequisites for Community Development," _International Review of Community Development_, Vol. 6 (1960).

Stock, Ernest. "Grass-Roots Politics--Israeli Style," _Midstream_, XII, 6 (June-July 1966).

Tanne, David. "Housing in Israel--Planning and Performance," _Public Administration in Israel and Abroad, 1964_, 5, Jerusalem, 1965.

Taylor, Carl C. "Community Development Programs and Methods," _Community Development Review_, Vol. 3 (December 1956).

Ten Have, T.T. _De Wetenschap der Sociale Agogie_. Groningen, 1962.

Tumin, Melvin M. "Some Social Requirements for Effective Community Development," _Community Development Review_, No. 11 (December 1958).

Turner, John B., ed. _Neighborhood Organization for Community Action_. New York: National Association of Social Workers, 1968.

BIBLIOGRAPHY

United Nations. "Policy Issues Concerning the Future Evolution
of Community Development." Unpublished draft prepared by
the Regional and Community Development Staff, April 1967
(67-47750).

Van Beugen, M. Sociale Technologie. Assen: Van Gorum & Co.,
1968.

Verner, Coolie. "The Community Development Process," Community
Development Review, Vol. 6, No. 1 (March 1961).

Viteles, Harry. A History of the Cooperative Movement in Israel.
London: Vallentine-Mitchell, 1967.

Vogel, R., and Oel, P. Gemeinde und Gemeinschaftshadeln: Zur
Analyse der Begriffe, Community Organization und Community
Development. Stuttgart: W. Kohlhammer Verlag, 1966.

Vroemen, J.J.G.M. "Het Werken aan de Samenleving: Verkenning
van een Terrein," NIMO Bulletin, No. 1 (January 1967).

Warren, Roland L. The Community in America. Chicago: Rand
McNally and Co., 1963.

__________, and Hyman, Herbert H. "Purposive Community Change in
Consensus and Dissensus Situations," Community Mental Health
Journal, Vol. 2, No. 4 (Winter 1967).

Weima, J. "Authoritarianism, Religious Conservatism and Socio-
Centered Attitudes in Roman Catholic Groups," Human Relations,
Vol. 18, No. 3 (August 1965).

Weingrod, Alex. Israel: Group Relations in a New Society.
London: Pall Mall Press, 1965.

__________. Reluctant Pioneers: Village Development in Israel.
Ithaca, N.Y.: Cornell University Press, 1966.

Weiss, Szewach. "Local Government in Israel: A Study of Its
Leadership." English summary of unpublished Ph.D. disserta-
tion, Department of Political Science, Hebrew University of
Jerusalem, December 1968.

Willner, Dorothy. "Politics and Change in Israel: The Case of
Land Settlement," Human Organization, Vol. 24, No. 1 (Spring
1965).

Zald, Mayer N. "Organizations as Polities: An Analysis of Community Organization Agencies," Social Work, Vol. 11, No. 4
(October 1966).

Zwanikken, Willem A.C. Community Development in The Netherlands:
    NIMO. The Hague, 1967.

________. "The Netherlands Institute of Community Development,"
    Community Development Journal, No. 6 (April 1967).

DATE DUE

GAYLORD · PRINTED IN U.S.A.